Primordial Characters

Primordial Characters

Rodney Needham

UNIVERSITY PRESS OF VIRGINIA
CHARLOTTESVILLE

THE UNIVERSITY PRESS OF VIRGINIA
Copyright © 1978 by the Rector and Visitors
of the University of Virginia

First published 1978

Frontispiece: Pinnacle from the chapel, Merton College, Oxford, now
at the University of Virginia. (Photograph by Margaret Williamson.)

Library of Congress Cataloging in Publication Data

Needham, Rodney.
Primordial characters.
Bibliography: p. 79
Includes index.
1.   Ethnopsychology—Addresses, essays, lectures.
2.   Imagination—Addresses, essays, lectures. I.   Title.
GN502.N43   301.2′1   78–17230   ISBN 0–8139–0774–8

Printed in the United States of America

To the memory of
H. V. D. Dyson
1896–1975

Contents

Preface   ix
Acknowledgments   xi

Prologue   1

Primary Factors   3
Synthetic Images   23
Evasive Fantasies   51

Select Bibliography   79
Index   85

Preface

THE LECTURES that make up this minor volume were delivered at the University of Virginia in September 1977 at the kind instance of the Committee on Comparative Study of Individual and Society and under the aegis of the Center for Advanced Studies.

The text is virtually unchanged, so that the rather schematic nature of the exposition has also been retained. The lectures were designed for a certain occasion and setting, with a cultivated but not necessarily professional audience in mind, and they are pitched at what I thought would be an appropriate tone and level of argument.

Rather than clutter the pages with references, and thus impede the fluency of the case as I tried to present it, I have appended a select bibliography to the extensive terrain through which the trail of my discourse runs. I should like however to state in advance my appreciation to Charles Rycroft for the stimulus provided by a number of passages in his article on Freud and the imagination. I have been particularly challenged, and I hope to agreeable effect, by his contention that "there are intrinsic, inherent limits to the amount that can be said about the imagination in general and . . . much of what can be said can only be stated in negative terms."

The work is dedicated to the memory of the late Hugo Dyson, sometime Fellow of Merton, in grateful recollection of the diffident charity with which, thirty years ago, he interviewed a distraught ex-infantryman and judged, on little more basis perhaps than compassion, that to admit him might not disgrace a proud Oxford college.

All Souls College, Oxford
October 1977

Acknowledgments

I AM GREATLY obliged to the Committee on Comparative Study of Individual and Society and the Center for Advanced Studies, University of Virginia, for the invitation to deliver these lectures, and especially to Mr. R. S. Khare for the indefatigable attention with which he made the arrangements and superintended their execution throughout. For generous hospitality and colleaguely support I am exceedingly grateful to the members of the Department of Anthropology under the chairmanship of Mr. R. Wagner. Among those who honored the lectures with their attendance, and instructed me afterwards with their comments and advice, I recall with particular pleasure Messrs. D. R. Barker, T. Caplow, F. M. Denny, D. L. Germino, J. N. Hartt, F. L. Richardson, and W. H. Sokel. To the many others at Charlottesville who made me welcome, and my return to the University so memorable, I offer my warmest thanks and recognition.

The photograph of the pinnacle from Merton College, Oxford, that supplies the motif to the frontispiece has been kindly furnished by Dr. Margaret Williamson of Mary Washington College, Virginia.

Primordial Characters

Prologue

FIFTY YEARS ago Alfred North Whitehead came to Mr. Jefferson's university to deliver the lectures that were published as *Symbolism: Its Meaning and Effect*. I have had that enigmatic and provocative work before my mind as I prepared the addresses that I am honored to be invited to offer you now. My concerns, in the topics that I shall take up, are essentially in accord with those of Whitehead, and I shall be flattered if the connection is conceded.

There is another link over the past half century that I should like to make. Whitehead's book opens with a dedication to the Commonwealth of Virginia. It is a page of rhapsody to the great experience that it is for an Englishman to cross the borders of Virginia, and to the romance of the name and of the conjoined history it represents. Twenty-one years have passed since I felt that experience for the first time and was introduced to the urbane civility and the ordered charms of the University of Virginia. Only a few years ago I was much gratified by the prospect of remaining with you in what is the nearest ambience in the United States to that of Oxford. The pinnacle from Merton chapel, set up in 1927 behind Pavilion VI, stands for very much more to me, in that place, than I could briefly disclose in these few lines. (To begin with, William Berkeley, a resolute and humane governor of Virginia in his first administration of 1641–52, was a Fellow of Merton.) I hope the lectures that are to follow will lead you to discern something of the meaning and effect of that perduring stone, compact with common values and aspirations; and also to see how it, in its turn, can serve as a symbolic guide to other vectors of the imagination.

As for the tenor of the lectures, the general line they pursue can be traced back in earlier publications of mine over quite a span of years, and it will be more or less familiar to my pupils at Oxford and in the United States. What I am trying to do now is to compose the interests and intimations thus expressed into a coherent, if summary, account of certain intrinsic characteristics of human consciousness. At some points the argument can rely on work already done, especially in my monograph on belief; at other places I can only allude to studies that I have undertaken but that I have not yet had the opportunity to prepare for publication. For the most part, however, I deal with matters that will be familiar to any reflective person; and although the best proofs would be likely to be rather technical, as for example in the analysis of prescriptive systems, I have tried to cast the lectures in a form that will make no such exacting demands. Certainly I shall be disappointed if only anthropologists are swayed by the ideas, however vague and insecure they may be, that I indicate in the course of these intermittent occasions. You will find in any case that as matters become more interesting I shall go considerably beyond what I can be sure of professionally. Some will presumably think that I go too far; but then that is precisely what I take to be an investigator's task and his calling.

Primary Factors

No NUDE, however abstract, should fail to arouse in the spectator some vestige of erotic feeling," Kenneth Clark has written, "and if it does not do so, it is bad art and false morals." In a similar vein, and in the terms that are more directly pertinent to the theme of these lectures, I should declare that no humane discipline, however rigorous, should fail to evoke from the student some sharper sense of the quandary of human existence; and if it does not do this it is trivial scholarship and morally insignificant.

Social anthropology, to take the widest exercise of humane comparativism, might claim the best authority to bring us to terms with ourselves and with the conditions of our lives; but at the same time it faces the severest tests of any humanistic study, and also the greatest resistance. Durkheim encountered something of this at the end of the last century. He was trying to establish sociology as an independent subject, and he achieved what in retrospect appears a striking academic success, but at a moral plane his ideas met considerable disfavor. If institutions exerted an independent constraint on men, and in the pervasive way claimed by Durkheim, then, it was thought, the moral autonomy of individual men was reduced or undermined. The objection was not based on sound argument, but the resistance demonstrates, even if negatively, my initial point. An academic discipline may be wholly admirable for its rigor and depth, or for its technical resources and analytical capacity, but if it is to make an impact on people's minds it must have a certain metaphysical implication: that is, it must be capable of suggesting something about the grand themes of consciousness, will, freedom, and the true character of man.

One cannot always see what exactly is the appeal, in any of these regards, of some subjects which have made such an impression but which most of those who are affected cannot well understand. Black holes are very much in fashion at the moment, and the latest opinions on quarks are also news, but the popularity of these topics in the Sunday newspapers does not much depend on a public understanding of general relativity or particle physics, nor indeed on any detached concern for the advance of science. No doubt many factors play their parts — a fascination with the ultimate, perhaps, or the lure of unbounded power — but at the center of them, I suppose, is the question of man's place in the vast implacable scheme of the universe. Much the same appears to be true of the popular interest in animal behavior. It is not so much the intrinsic factuality of bees dancing, sticklebacks skirmishing, or chimpanzees making tools that appeals: it is the possibility of interpreting the actions of other species in human terms, and by reflection also the actions of humans in terms thought to be common to other creatures. Certainly it is a great puzzle that people in complex technological societies should be so attracted by the occasion to see themselves as naked apes or indolent lions or bewildered rats; but it is true all the same, I think, that people are powerfully inclined to make imaginative assimilations between other species and themselves (a matter to which we shall return), and that they tend to draw moral conclusions about human nature from these dramatic comparisons.

Yet it is an interesting fact that men have not on the whole put the observation of their fellow men to such didactic use. It is a frequent report from different parts of the world that tribes call themselves alone by the arrogant title "man," and that they refer to neighboring peoples as monkeys or crocodiles or malign spirits. When European voyagers explored the world, they often enough had a clear eye for physique, dress, and habitations, but they more often had a distorted or derogatory view of the moral aspects of exotic peoples. Typically, these strange societies had no religion, or no law, or no idea of the family, or not even a true form of language to qualify them as truly human. There were admirable exceptions, of course, but in general a fair contrast can be delineated: strange peoples might be naturalistically observed—like the form, plumage, and nests of birds—but they were not objects for moral sympathy or emulation. If the observation was taken to be morally instructive, the lesson drawn was that the observers were supreme, if not incomparable, in every virtue.

With the Enlightenment, this stance began to alter, and a humanistic ethnography was developed that has a direct descent down to modern social anthropology, but the earlier imbalance is still evident: ornithology, for instance, is immensely more advanced than is the natural history of mankind. There are, admitted, a number of ethnographic studies of individual peoples which as feats of descriptive integration can match studies of other species, but in the main our knowledge of the varieties of mankind and their forms of life is deplorably thin, patchy, and unreliable. This state of affairs is itself a social fact, and it tells us something about the impulsions of men as students of other men. The comparative study of human beings was for a long time not attractive as a scientific undertaking; and a possible inference is that it was not better developed because, paradoxically, it was not expected to provide a humane metaphysics. That is, if men were perplexed about the meaning of existence, or the essential nature of their kind, or the right way of life, they were not immediately persuaded that the answers were to be found among foreigners.

Conversely, it can be argued, the rapid professional development of social anthropology since the latter part of the nineteenth century has been achieved on condition that the subject should actually abjure any moral or metaphysical concern. The succession of theoretical fashions in the course of a century — evolutionism, diffusionism, functionalism, scientism, structuralism — were by design increasingly detached and abstract, constantly relying on operational metaphors borrowed from one or another branch of natural science. No wonder that the public, concomitantly estranged by a subject that grew more and more technical and remote, became hardly more inclined to turn to anthropology for a measure of their own concerns.

These days, when we can already look on structuralism as a passing mode in the metaphor of inquiry (as distinct from the antique abstractions from which it had its limited efficacy), things are supposed to be different. We have shifted, it is said, from function to meaning. But essentially the shift is simply that, instead of looking for the uses or the causal connections of institutions, we try better to grasp what alien ideas and practices mean to those whose lives are framed by them. This is all well enough, but it is still no more than a precondition for the elaboration of anything like an empirical philosophy, by which I mean a comparative discipline that might serve as a guide to the interpretation of human experience.

There are two main reasons, among a number, for this state of affairs. One is that the development of a science of man was carried out in the wrong direction: that is, from large-scale to contextual, from the general to the particular, instead of the other way round. From the eighteenth century, the heyday of "systems," down to the twentieth, theoretical emphasis has been placed on the discovery of laws and, latterly, structures; whereas a necessarily prior consideration has always been an account of the properties of those institutions that are governed by the hypothetical laws or that are structurally interconnected as systems. Thus the ambition of anthropologists was to explain "religion" or "the state" or "kinship" or "law" as universal phenomena, rather than to discover what were the definitive properties or components of the social facts that were classed together under such indiscriminate labels. Only quite recently have we got to the point, and by conceptual analysis rather than by improved ethnography, of isolating the elementary phenomena and abstractions that variously combine into institutions.

The other reason, which is connected with the former, is that anthropologists have concentrated on the study of social systems, collective practices, and ideologies, not on the essential characteristics of human beings, that is, on human nature. This topic was for millennia a constant preoccupation of philosophers and aphorists, but as soon as something like a comparative science of man was founded, oddly enough, human nature was relegated to a background of unexamined premises. Western anthropologists, instead of asking what were in fact the essential, and hence universal, capacities and characteristics of man, took it for granted that they already knew what these were, and that the vocabularies of their own languages provided them with entirely adequate means of description and analysis. Again, only quite recently, and once more by conceptual analysis (that is, philosophically rather than by ethnographic investigation), has it been taken as an empirical question to determine whether all men everywhere can equally be said to love or to feel awe or to believe. Yet as soon as a comparative study of any concept of the inner life is carried out, it becomes the more obvious that the disparities among psychological and epistemological vocabularies in different traditions pose fundamental problems. Either they are all correct as objective discriminations, in which case human nature is as infinitely malleable as the vocabularies are various; or else universal correspondences can be established among the vocabularies, in which case certain capacities and ideas are essential to a definition of man while the others are idiosyncratic constructs that label nothing real. Now cultures are created by human beings, and, in spite of the fact that collective representations and individual capacities or conceptions are of different orders, there must be an intrinsic connection between them. We have done quite well in coming to terms with social facts, but these still cannot be satisfactorily understood unless we can link them to the human powers that generated them; and we cannot possibly do that until we have identified the capacities, proclivities, and constraints that universally make up human nature.

A convenient phrase by which to refer to such determinants is "primary factors of experience," and it is possible

to discern quite a range of them. Let me begin a quick survey by adducing some of the standard components of symbolism and metaphysics. I am afraid that it is not feasible to
make a factual demonstration of each point, and I shall have
to ask you to take the ethnographic evidences on trust.

Early Greek thought, as Geoffrey Lloyd has fascinatingly
shown, relied extensively on physical contrasts such as hot
and cold, wet and dry, in making not only physical judgments but moral estimations as well. This resort to material
properties in order to assess human virtues, the prevalence
of which has been emphasized by Cassirer and others, is
common among ourselves. We speak of someone as being
hardheaded, and of someone else as being softhearted; a
contrast in psychic resilience between the sexes is phrased
by saying that men are (or ought to be) hard, whereas
women are (or are found appealing as) soft; people are distinguished, or an individual is characterized at different
stages of his life, as toughminded and tenderminded; and
so on through a series of what are superficially regarded as
metaphors. I am not denying, of course, that they are metaphors. What I want to stress is that the widespread incidence of such figures of speech in differing linguistic
traditions points to some fundamental influence to which
men tend to be subject in articulating their experience.

Another prominent kind of sensory factor is color, a
subject on which also a great deal has been written, so that
I need make in this instance too only a brief allusion to its
relevance. Two points are central. First, that men resort to
colors in distinguishing or characterizing all sorts of things:
castes, points of the compass, deities, moods, professions,
and so on. Second, that again and again they make use of
the same colors. A great many hues can be distinguished in

the visible spectrum, color vocabularies are often extensive, and materials for fabricating a number of the colors distinguished can usually be found. Yet with an arresting frequency, as has been pointed out by de Vries and others, it is the triad of red, white, and black that is singled out in order to convey symbolic significance. Here again the contrast between the wide span of sensory stimuli and the extreme economy of the symbolism points to a highly selective influence.

Much the same is true of numbers. First, that in ascribing a systematic importance to things, or in marking distinctions, men constantly resort to numbers. Thus we find around the world, as Allendy has best described, classifications that are partitioned according to definitive or "sacred" numbers; and these numbers tend to be small integers, such as two, three, four, seven, nine. Typical examples are the fourfold division of society or of a city, or the contrast commonly marked by associating men with one number (e.g., four) and women with another (e.g., three). In some cases, which are all the more remarkable when arithmetical ability is not much developed, a more general discrimination is made by reference to odd numbers and even numbers: for instance, there are indications that among the Nyoro odd numbers tend to be associated with the feminine, contingent, extraordinary, and mystical status, whereas even numbers are associated with masculine, regularity, formal action, and secular status.

Among sensory perceptions that are used widely for symbolic ends is sound. There is a special interest in one type of sound that is highly comparable among different cultures, since it is not necessarily connected with melody or rhythm or pitch. This is percussion, and it seems that

this quality of sound is significantly associated with transition from one state to another or with mediating between
one category and another, such as earthly and spiritual. By
means of bells, gongs, drums, rattles, and numerous other
instruments and devices, percussion is accorded a singular
place among sounds; and in the decade since the association
with transition was first noted, the implicit significance
has been confirmed by one ethnographer after another. The
interpretation may in due course have to be changed or re-
fined, and the etiology has not yet been established, but it
looks as if percussive sound can also be listed among the
primary factors that I have set out to exemplify.

You will have noticed that I have not defined the term: I
have not stated in what sense these phenomena are primary,
nor in what manner they are factors. For the moment, I
want to give you merely a rough idea of what I am talking
about, so that we can press on with the general viewpoint
that I wish to present. Two points should however be made
about the examples that I have sketchily indicated just now.
First, that the factors are heterogeneous: the contrast of
textures pertains to touch, colors to vision; numbers are
abstractions, percussion depends on hearing. Second, they
are vehicles for significance but they do not convey explicit universal meanings. So if such factors of experience
are primary, in some sense, and have a global incidence, it
does not follow that they will have any further semantic
properties in common. What could perhaps be said at present is that they are phenomena of the same order, and this
order is defined by simplicity and immediacy.

It would be absurd, at this stage of inquiry, to draw too
much on analogies with natural science, but there is at least
an apparent similarity that lends some encouragement:

namely, the possibility that such primary factors, or elementary constituents of culture, may play a part in theoretical advance like that of elements in chemistry or particles in physics. Moreover, the notion continues and intensifies a line of analysis in anthropology since the last century: from elementary forms to elementary structures. In this theoretical development the emphasis was indeed on the discovery of ultimately simple social facts, but at the wrong scale, since the forms and structures postulated were actually complex entities such as totemic cults or social systems organized by a variety of terminologies and rules of marriage and descent. By contrast, the primary factors that I have alluded to, whether or not they can be regarded as truly elementary, are at least far more simple: hardness (as of stone), the color red (as of blood), the number nine (that it can be broken down arithmetically is irrelevant, for this fact may or may not have a collective significance), the immediacy of the clash of a gong.

How many such factors there may be is a matter for empirical inquiry, but we can make in advance some quite optimistic assertions on this count. First, that among the tens of thousands of entities and attributes which are denoted by their languages and are thereby apt for selection as elementary vehicles of meaning, each culture has chosen, as it were, only a very economical number of items. Second, that if we compare schemes of symbolic classification around the world, as for instance in *Right & Left*, we find that the same things (in a pragmatic sense) recur again and again. So it is justifiable to conceive that there may be a more or less limited number of primary factors: not an absolute figure, but a recognizable range beyond which individual cultures may then elaborate their own idiosyncratic semantic units. The number of factors could even be quite high, yet our method of investigation need not in principle be affected. Given that it is feasible to isolate any primary factor, the number of additional ones has no operational importance: it will be merely a matter of establishing one after another. This undertaking, given the premise that they are heterogeneous, cannot be deductive: the task depends on patient isolation and comparison. If the total number of factors were to turn out to run into the hundreds, or for that matter into the thousands, we should simply have to come to terms with that fact and accept the proliferation as characteristic of the representation of human consciousness.

But I do not think the total (in the flexible sense I have just mentioned) is at all high. On the contrary, the indications provided by world ethnography are that in general, not only in individual cultures, the range of primary factors is very economical. We can conjecture a reason that it should be so: namely, that a restricted number of semantic elements is more manageable and effective as a code. It may even be that for this reason the economy proved an adaptive advantage in the cultural evolution of our species. There is another reason, more fundamental and considerably more speculative. I shall come to this interesting guesswork later, when I shall try to draw some inferences about imaginative consciousness and collective representations.

For the present, the empirical point to take is that it is by reference to such features, whether or not we call them primary factors, that it is possible to do social anthropology at all. It is by virtue of such natural resemblances among men, in their various modes of constructing and interpreting reality, that it is possible to compare one tradition with another, or for an outsider to comprehend an exotic form of civilization. Academic anthropologists seem to take it rather as a matter of course that they should direct, and even on occasion correct, studies of cultures with which they may have no direct acquaintance and of which even their reading knowledge may be limited indeed. How then is this done? Certainly not by what is commonly referred to as anthropological "theory," but in the main, I think, by having learned (even if not always explicitly) what to look for and even what to expect. In these respects we are identifying the characteristic features not just of individual cultures but of human culture; and any phenomena that can enable us to do this ought surely to be made the objects of special and concerted investigation. Hence, I propose, the basic importance of research into primary factors as semantic units in our representation of human experience.

You will have been thinking, of course, that it is not by such units alone that we apprehend or construct anything. Words are connected by grammar, institutions are connected by laws, events are connected by causal or correlative links. What makes a systematic grasp of things possible is relationship, and an obvious query is whether there are also relations that naturally inhere in the formation of collective representations and can hence be regarded as factors of the kind we are considering.

Certainly there are. An excellent example is provided by the topic of lateral symbolism — right and left — and we can start just by looking at the way you button your shirts. The men's button to the right, and right-handedly; the women's (unless they go to Brooks Brothers) button to the left, and as though they were left-handed. This is one everyday instance of a worldwide opposition of values in

which right stands for men, and left for women. Analogi-
cally, right is often associated also with the sun, strength,
hardness, and many other superior qualities, whereas left
may be associated with the moon, weakness, softness, and
so on. The particular values that are partitioned in agreement with the symbolism of the sides, in one culture or
another, can vary: for instance, the sun may be regarded as
feminine (as the Purum do) and hence be associated with
the left, while the moon goes with masculine and the right.
But there are two impressive constants in this example. One
is that right and left are universally employed as symbols;
the other is that the contrast of values in this form of symbolism exhibits a relation of binary opposition that is resorted to by men everywhere in exploiting the simplest
form of classification.

The relation of opposition is itself only one of a severely
limited number of formal relations by which semantic units,
in the first place, are articulated. I need not expatiate on
them, for they are familiar in traditional logic as symmetry,
transitivity, and correlation. These relations are not merely
constructs designed for the security of philosophical
thought, nor is it adventitious or tautological that they can
be discerned in all kinds of institutions. They are intrinsic
to the institutions, and in analyzing social facts by reference
to such formal abstractions we are establishing a correspondence between the exigencies of our thought and the
determinants of cultural institutions. I realize that these
are compressed assertions of large matters, and there is not
the occasion now to provide ethnographical illustrations;
so I must ask you to accept that in the practice of structural
analysis (especially in the field of prescriptive alliance)
the relations of symmetry and transitivity, in their various

modes and combinations, have proved to have a remarkable elucidatory value.

Last among the formal constraints that I am rapidly collocating here, as a resource in the interpretation of social facts, is that of logical possibility. By this I do not advert to modes of inference or canons of validity or styles of rational cogitation; but simply to the general consequence that, given certain social facts as premises, only certain social forms or courses of action may be possible. For the anthropologist an obvious field of evidence is that of descent systems. A matter that has much impressed comparativists since 1724, when Lafitau found congruencies between the social organization of the native Americans and that of the peoples of the Old Testament, is that there are many striking similarities, both in system and in detail, among descent systems in the most far-separated parts of the globe. In the past hundred years especially, as ethnographic knowledge has advanced, the similarities have appeared more and more marked; so that rather than discovering a proliferation of idiosyncratic and disparate systems, social anthropology can with increasing confidence identify certain common attributes that readily permit the analysis and comparison of even the most exotic and hitherto unknown descent systems from anywhere in the world.

An expectable consequence of this much success has been the temptation to classify the systems into distinct types according to whatever features were taken to be definitive, and since the latter part of the nineteenth century this emphasis on a sociological typology has been very much in vogue. It did not prove to be scientifically productive, however, and a subtler style of comparison was introduced in 1917 by Lowie, who argued that the emphasis should be not on types and on systems named after particular tribes but instead on the principles that articulated the social forms defined by descent. This was a genial clarification, even though it had little effect on received ideas, and all that was needed theoretically was to say something about the principles themselves. A few years ago I tried to do so, and came to an encouragingly simple conclusion: namely, that, given two procreative sexes, only six elementary modes of descent were logically possible, and that of these six only four were pragmatically feasible as ways of organizing social life. What I think can then be claimed is that it is by virtue of these principles that descent systems are so very alike and so readily comparable: in other words, that the social forms are universally determined by a restricted number of relational factors that express logical constraints and alternatives.

There are other phenomena, proclivities, constraints, and determinants that could be instanced as primary factors, but I trust these examples will have given an idea of their generality and of their simple character. You will appreciate of course that these are the very attributes that one would look for a priori in seeking the universal grounds of effective comparison; yet for the most part the postulated factors have been arrived at not deductively but by intense collation of ethnographic evidences. They have moreover certain other attributes that one could not well have deduced: in the first place the heterogeneity that I have already mentioned. A more important attribute, because more fundamental, is that they are not consciously selected or fabricated; that is, they are independent of the will. This in its turn makes it easier to grasp a further attribute: namely, that they are nonsystematic, in that there are no necessary interconnections and that one factor can change or be absent without affecting the others. It is no wonder, therefore, that forms of civilization, even though highly comparable by reference to primary factors in general, should nevertheless exhibit an extreme elaboration and a capacity for perpetual change. This after all is just what we should expect of the relation between factors and forms.

No doubt you will have been struck by the implication that the idea of primary factors rests on something like a doctrine of "natural kinds": that we have been dealing with natural resemblances in the forms of perceptions, foci of attention, and implicit logical conditions that are given in nature and in human nature. This is indeed a doctrine that is consistent with the existence of primary factors; and to the extent that the factors are conceded to exist, the doctrine of natural kinds is confirmed by them. Correlatively, it might be contended that the primary factors correspond in certain senses to what are traditionally known as "innate ideas," though this position is rather more difficult to maintain without extensive qualification. Or else you may find it a helpful analogy, within its obvious limits, to conceive the repertory of primary factors as resembling an ideal language, constituting what used to be called a "real character." The patent difference of course is that the terms of an ideal language are intended to carry definite and invariant meanings; whereas the generative capacity of primary factors is precisely that they are capable of conveying an infinite variety of meanings.

On the other hand, although it would be exaggerating to refer to it as a grammar, there is a combinative tendency among certain factors which thereby constitute not so much systems, let alone necessary connections, as complexes. A

familiar example is the body of images and organizing ideas
that make up shamanism, a mystical institution that exhibits, as Eliade has established in his classic study, a striking
constancy of form that is practically universal. Another example, which though not universal has nevertheless an impressive historical and territorial span, is that of the custom
of blood offering to a thunder deity that is practiced in
Malaya, Borneo, and the Philippines; this is a form of sacrifice in which some nine or ten discrete features, the presence
of none being entailed by any others, cohere remarkably
into a ritual complex that is almost identical among culturally very different peoples. As a third example let me
mention, though I have not yet been able to publish my
findings, the image of the half man that is found all over the
world and that also appears to be a complex constituted
by primary factors. So the task of comparativism, on the
scale of worldwide ethnography, is not only to isolate individual factors and their operation, but also to delineate
the symbolic complexes that are constituted by these factors
in the collective representation of human experience.

To the historian of ideas it will be apparent that in certain general regards this enterprise resumes the attempts of
Bastian, a century ago, to list the *Elementargedanken* of mankind. There are however quite trenchant differences, both
of conception and especially of method, between Bastian's
discontinued venture and the undertaking that has been the
subject of this lecture. This contrast (for what it is worth
by comparison with the recognition due to a worthy prede-
cessor) will become plainer in the second lecture, when
we shall work out a factorial analysis of one of the most
dramatic complexes to have preoccupied men's imaginations.

Let me for the present conclude this introductory address by reverting for a moment to the considerations with which we began. I alluded then to the themes of consciousness, will, freedom, and the true nature of man; and it is to these themes that the topics I have so sketchily treated can nevertheless be related. No doubt as much could be said, by the employment of sufficient sophistry, in the scrutiny of any human activity; but there is no need to resort to special pleading, for the ethnographic evidences speak plainly enough for themselves. I should stress, also, that the very great differences among ethnographers tend to preclude conceptual predispositions that would have brought their testimonies into a tendentious agreement that happened to suit my purpose. So far as objectivity can be conceded to social facts, the primary factors that I have indicated appear to have a real character. How, then, do they impinge on the grand themes I have just recalled?

One of the main concerns of traditional philosophy was the establishment of the categories of understanding, in the sense that these constituted ultimate predicates in whatever men chose to say about themselves and the world. This ambition has become harder to sustain, especially as scholars such as Benveniste have come to terms with the implicit categories of non–Indo-European languages. It no longer seems so practicable to isolate a definite number of adamantine categories that are apt to the analysis of propositions in Ewe as well as in classical Greek, in Chinese as well as in English. Nevertheless, the impulsion to seek ultimate predicates is an ineradicable motive in assessing the constructions that men place upon their experience. If we ask questions about consciousness and the other themes, we are committed to assessing the character of the terms in which we represent experience and pose the questions. Now our epistemological categories are by definition cognitive, and they are framed by the distinctive forms of our language, so it is not to be expected that they will accommodate other cultural modes, metaphysical and linguistic, of taking account of man and his place in the world. What can be suggested, however, is that primary factors, in their simplicity and their immediacy, may play in imaginative consciousness a part similar to that of ultimate predicates in epistemology. Whether they are viewed as proclivities or as constraints, or whether any particular factor has the one character or the other, they are still determinants; and to the extent that they exert a directive influence they set limits to our power of representation.

You will remember of course that I am speaking so far of collective representations only, and that it is these that make up the empirical evidence against which the suggestions offered in this lecture are to be tested. It is consistent with the autonomous nature of collective representations that the primary factors are not products of the will, any more than are the senses and apperceptions and mental capacities of which ex hypothesi they are elementary manifestations. This need be no more repugnant to the values of individualism than is the realization that our reasoning is governed by the constraints of an informal logic, or that our perceptions are limited by the powers of our senses. But to concede any directive influence means that we are not so free and not so individual as we might be, nor so much perhaps as we thought we were.

Synthetic Images

I HAVE EVER beleeved, and doe now know, that there are Witches." It is little more than three hundred years since a humane and learned doctor, Sir Thomas Browne, made that decided declaration. Some years later even he acted as medical witness for the prosecution in sending two old women to their deaths for the crime of witchcraft. Since his day we in the West have not been free of the obsession, for even when the last poor creature had been burnt or put to the test, the power of the collective representation survived. Historians reverted again and again to the trials and the edicts and the fulminations; folklorists traced the continued expression of ideas about witchcraft into modern society; eccentrics claimed to be, or tried to be, witches and formed themselves into covens on desolate farms and in sedate suburbs; and the anthropologists, of course, made it into one of the stock and indispensable topics of their subject.

In these regards it can be said that we are still in the power of the idea of witchcraft, just as we resort to its dramatic power in our metaphors of moral condemnation and political castigation. If it is objected that we do not actually do anything about it, this is true in the sense that we do not arrest and torture those whom we call witches, and that we do not presume to be witches those who are the victims of witch hunts. But we do not have to do and think so in order to conform to a collective representation; for neither did most people, I can conceive, in the days when such things really were done. It was the church and the state that provided the authority and the punitive means: they were the sustainers of the institution, and in this respect were parts of it. We cannot say that the authorities responded to the common conviction that there were witches, for to the common people the fearsome notion of witchcraft was not a spontaneous apprehension but had all the autonomy, generality, and coercive force of a social fact. And if we were to say that they believed in the dread powers of witchcraft, and hence collaborated in the gruesome procedures by which the authorities tried to extirpate witches, we should be on even shakier ground. In spite of the volume of contemporary reports, we do not know what the greater number of the populace believed (on the assumption that we have a clear idea of what "believe" means), but only that the collective representation was in force.

We can well conclude, moreover, that people in the past no more positively acquiesced in the execution of witches, or played any other deliberate part in the enactment of the representation, than do we today in the operation of the institutions that govern our own lives, even when the instruments of state are called representative or the corporations are called public. If we agree that people really did think there were witches, this does not justify us in imputing any particular state of mind to them. There have been crazes and scares, but these are not generically characteristic of the institution. We ourselves know, just as objectively (let us say), that hundreds of thousands of people are killed and maimed on the turnpikes; and although we regard this as deplorable, and try to make turnpikes less dangerous or to avoid the dangers if we travel on them, the knowledge and the consequent precautions do not argue for any special kind of judgment or apprehension that is distinctively associated with turnpikes. Indeed, this is much what we find when we read ethnographic accounts of societies where witches are just as real, and also just as normal an aspect of everyday life, as are turnpikes to us. There are witches, all right, and people rely on regular precautions and techniques in order to cope with them.

I have been stressing the points in these preliminary remarks in order to throw into contrast the aspect of witchcraft that I think really important and that is to be the subject of this lecture. The more normal the idea of witchcraft is taken to be, in a society where it is in force, the more striking is that aspect. The less we assume that the institution of witchcraft involves a special inner state, the more readily we shall be able to analyze the power and persistence of the complex that defines the institution. If, on the other hand, we regard the institution of witchcraft merely as a cognitive aberration, a kind of collective nightmare that can be exorcised by science, then I think we are missing some of its most interesting and instructive features. Actually, the case I intend to make first is that social anthropology, in the ways it has approached witchcraft, has tended to pass over these features and at the same time has not made a good scientific argument in any other respect.

Difficulty began with the definition of a witch, and sporadically a fair amount of literary energy went into discriminating between witch and sorcerer, the former work-

ing by some intrinsic property, the latter by recourse to
material means; then in deciding whether in a certain society
a mystical practitioner was the one or the other, or maybe
both at the same time; and then in qualifying propositions
about witchcraft according to whether a witch or a sorcerer
was in question, not to mention the alternative statuses of
wizard, magician, conjuror, and so on. Moreover, beyond
the range of the English words there were the numerous
terms in other languages that were indifferently translated
as "witch" and the like, and each of these constituted a
semantic problem that did not readily conduce to comparative generalizations. And against this tangled background anthropologists still found it possible to speak of
"genuine" witches or of witches "proper," to differ over
whether witches were essentially immoral, and, expectably
enough, to become diverted by one new typological consideration after another according to the ethnographic data
adduced or the cast put upon them by the anthropological
commentator. At the end of the day, it remains a question if
there is yet a definition of a witch that is agreeable, in the
rigorous acceptation seemingly required, to anthropologists
as a body. If you ask whether that really matters, the answer
is that it depends on the theoretical or comparative propositions that have "witch" as their subject. We shall come to
some of these in a moment. For the present occasion, I shall
give the word its common, or garden, meaning of someone
who causes harm to others by mystical means. If you are inclined to protest that this is altogether too rough and ready,
let me invite you to wait a little until I show that this
vagueness of definition has no importance for the purpose I
have in view.

You may, by the way, find it interesting to keep in mind

later a point about Germanic etymology. The English word *witch* comes from the Old English *wićće*, the feminine form of *wićća*, which is rendered as a male magician, sorcerer, or wizard, and this is the end of the trail, since the source of these words is not understood. But in German the equiva-lent *Hexe* comes from the Middle High German *hag*, meaning a "fence," "hedge," or "enclosure"; and the Icelandic *tūnriða*, witch, means literally a female "fence-rider." There is thus a connection, which will acquire its point as we proceed, between witches and boundaries. It would be instructive to learn if this association is to be found in other linguistic traditions.

Another preliminary matter that ought to be mentioned is the almost universal premise subscribed to by anthro-pologists, that witches do not really exist: that is, no human beings have the secret power to inflict harm or do evil as witches are supposed to do. This is a curious presumption, though I do not maintain that it has led to any pragmatic difficulty in the study of witchcraft. It is odd because it is a flagrant instance of sheer prejudice of the kind that anthro-pologists are usually careful to avoid when dealing with other mystical institutions. They do not as a rule begin by declaring that God does not exist or that ancestral spirits are merely imaginary or that the benefits of blessing are illusory. They say that these notions are to be treated as social facts, and that there is simply no need to pronounce on their truth or falsity. But in the case of witchcraft there is no such compunction: witches just do not exist, and the question posed is hence why men universally but mis-guidedly think that they do. I must say this strikes me as pure dogma. I myself have no idea, empirically, whether any human beings possess a secret capacity to inflict harm by

some immaterial and unseen means. This seems to me something of an open question. I have no evidence that there is
such a power, whether generic or confined to a minority of
individuals, and my inclination is to suspect that most
probably there is none. But the one thing I am sure of,
simply as a point of method, is that we ought not to base
our investigation into witchcraft on an unsure (even unexamined) premise, let alone the premise that the essential
attribute of witches — namely the malign power — does
not exist.

The standard concession to reality made by anthropologists is that the idea of witchcraft must be related, as
Philip Mayer has put it, to something real in human experience; but the next move is none the less to fall back on
another prejudice, namely, that the reality in question consists in social and psychological strains to which the postu-
lation of witchcraft is a social response. I am not saying
that correlations of the kind cannot be made (though what
they are worth is a different matter), but that the presumed
locus of the reality of witchcraft corresponds in the first
place to the sociological predilections of anthropologists.
An extreme expression of this leaning is to be seen in an
assertion, by two leading authorities, that sociological
analysis "must" be employed if we wish to develop ex-
planatory formulations which can subsume the facts from
more than one society.

However that may be, the notion that witchcraft accusations point to "weak spots in the social structure" has
had a considerable prevalence. Related propositions are
that the accusations derive from a conflict between ideal
and actual social relations; that they are a means to break
relationships that have become insupportable; or that they

act as a safety valve by which aggressive impulses are sub-
limated. The ethnographic accounts presented in these
terms may be very informative, and the focus on tensions
and strains can certainly contribute to a true description of
social life, but the approach is nevertheless subverted by a
number of considerations that cannot be countered by the
improvement of fieldwork.

First, it is tautological to say that witchcraft accusations
point to weak spots or to difficult relationships, for it is in
part the accusations themselves that characterize the spots
as weak or the relationships as uneasy. Moreover, what is
needed is an independent gauge of strength and smoothness
by which the ethnographer could assess these qualities in
the absence of their liability to accusations; but in the
nature of the case the possibility of correlating witchcraft
accusations and social vulnerability, as independent vari-
ables, cannot be had. And in any case a test by concomitant
variation is called for: to identify "strong" points in the
social structure and to check that they are free of witchcraft accusations; and to check the "weak" points and see
if they are regularly the targets of accusations. These however are tasks that in the main have not been carried out in
ethnographical analyses, and lacking their results we are
left without satisfactory empirical proof of the alleged
connection. Finally, even if the connection could be established in particular instances, the question would remain
whether the weak and difficult spots were so precisely because, for some other reason perhaps, they were conventionally regarded as the loci of witchcraft. This is a question
that applies similarly to the safety valve, or sublimation,
hypothesis, for we cannot know to what extent the tension
or the aggression is a product of the institution itself.

As matters stand, at any rate, I think it is true to say that no sociological or psychological explanation of the differential incidence of witchcraft accusations has been borne out empirically as a general proposition that is valid for witchcraft everywhere. Witches are neighbors, or else they are distant; they are relatives, or else they cannot be relatives; they are marginal, or else they are enemies within; they are lowly misfits, or else they are secure and prosperous just because of their witchcraft; they are so categorized that not everybody can be a witch, or else they are such that anyone may be a witch. Occasionally a sociological proposition is framed in even more detailed terms: for example, that witchcraft beliefs tend to be utilized in societies in which unilineal kinship principles are employed in the formation of local residential groups larger than the domestic household. The literature of anthropology is replete with propositions like these, each perhaps persuasive in its own ethnographic setting, but none survives as a key to the institution wheresoever it may be found. No wonder that a historian such as Trevor-Roper asserts that witchcraft beliefs are inseparable from the ideology of the time. But this conclusion does not allow for, even if it does not rule out, the comparativism that is proper to social anthropology and that alone may provide a general interpretation an institution that has such a global distribution. The historian's conclusion is the ethnographer's indispensable premise.

There is still one other kind of explanation, however, that seems to fare better and that is not cast in terms of jural institutions and social systems. This is the view that the idea of witchcraft provides a theory of misfortune. If that termite-riddled granary (the bane of anthropological examiners) falls on you and not on someone else, just as you happened to be sitting under it, the activity of a witch provides not only an answer to the question "Why me?" but a final and complete answer. Also it enables you to do something definite, dramatic, and perhaps personally advantageous about the source of your misfortune.

No doubt the institution of witchcraft does have these occasional uses, but they do not explain why it is that this particular institution is employed in order to explain misfortune. After all, there are many ways to do that. If misfortune strikes, you can blame an inscrutable god or capricious spirits; you can concede that it is the just retribution of your own sin, or else that it is the automatic consequence of some unintended fault; you can put it down to bad luck (if your culture happens to have this Germanic concept), or more calculatingly you can ascribe it to chance (though this is an even more difficult notion). Theories of these kinds are legion, they are found also in societies that ascribe misfortune to witchcraft as well, and even people obsessed by witches do not blame every misfortune on their malign intervention. Why then should people hold to a theory that places responsibility for their misfortunes on other people? From a pragmatic point of view, it does not even seem a particularly desirable theory. If people think they are afflicted by an inscrutable god, they can at least band together in an attempt to placate their divine scourge by communal means that do not foster suspicion and set them one against another. But to blame individual human beings for riddled posts or failing crops or the attacks of unpredictable wild animals seems the most self-damaging theory of any.

All the same, the idea is remarkably prevalent in history

and in world ethnography, and for all its apparent social disadvantages we have to accept that in fact this theory of blame is the way in which a great many peoples have chosen to think about the sources of their troubles. This fact in itself tells us something about the inclinations of human beings under stress, but I do not think the theory of misfortune hypothesis tells us anything interesting or revealing about the institution of witchcraft. In a sense, indeed, we might well not have expected it to do so, for this proposition too is tautologous by definition: ideas about witchcraft account for the blows of misfortune, after all, not for the blessings of comity.

It has taken me some little while to run through this essential introductory survey of the state of theory with regard to witchcraft, and as you see I cannot find that there is much in the way of positive results to report. This is not surprising, let alone dejecting, if only because it is a delusion to suppose that we shall do best at explaining widespread and constant social facts. We can do much better with limited and variant institutions, that is, when the weight of comparativism can least be brought to bear. If comparison is the characteristic method of social anthropology, it does not follow that we shall be very effective with it. At any rate, we have not in fact got very far in the scientific treatment of the idea of witchcraft.

It is against this background that I now want to turn to the features of witchcraft that earlier on I said struck me as interesting and as anthropologically neglected. I am not going to claim any great progress or revelation, and the matter is not one for decisive argument; but when we are so much baffled by an institution as we are in this case, an oblique attention to it, from another standpoint, may just make a difference. You will already be familiar with the features themselves, but it is perhaps when we think we are most familiar with a thing that a change of aspect can best disclose its further properties.

The aspect that I want to focus on is the image of the witch, and I shall try to make sense of its components by resort to what were introduced in the first lecture as primary factors of experience. There is, as you will see, no technique for doing this, and at points I have to rely on conjectures that are no more than plausible; but what follows is at any rate a way of thinking about witchcraft that may lead somewhere interesting.

The first reason for taking the image as the object of analysis, rather than the sociological matters that have hitherto preoccupied most anthropologists, is that amid a welter of contingent social facts (which, as we have found, have not been brought into a consistent theoretical order) this complex construction of the imagination displays a very remarkable constancy. I do not mean by this that the components of the image of the witch are always the same in number and character, from one tradition to another, but that there are characteristic features which combine polythetically (that is, by sporadic resemblances) to compose a recognizable imaginative definition of the witch.

Let us approach this representation by way of its moral component. The witch is said to do such horrible things as to eat children, practice cannibalism by secretly devouring people's organs, commit incest, and otherwise act in a vile and malevolent manner such as only the right-minded could imagine. (Eating children, incidentally, has a special vogue: Domitian charged Apollonius with it; the Romans accused the Christians; the Christians in turn the Jews.) Such par-

ticulars are infinitely elaborated on, but these are some of
the major attributes. Anthropologists have frequently re-
marked that such conduct is grossly abnormal, or shocking,
or contrary to decent norms; but I suggest that those com-
mentators are more exact who say that morally the witch is
the very opposite of the right values of society. This is not
a trite point of vocabulary, but it corresponds significantly
to the estimations of members of society. Typically, moral
evaluations are scalar, such that actions are judged as more
or less good, more or less bad. There are extreme instances
at the polar ends of the scale, but at one end these are hypothetical; even societies that recognize saints concede that
these exemplars have blemishes (as the saints themselves of
course have to insist) and are not absolutely good. It would
be both expectable and practicable, therefore, if societies
were to place witches at various points toward the op-
probrious end of the moral scale; certainly they would be
bad, but more or less bad, and this means that they would
be allowed to possess some virtues. But in fact the witch is
not given the benefit of this moral nicety: the witch is absolutely and irremediably evil, a real instance of the polar
type that merits utter condemnation. The witch's conduct
is not merely contrasted with the ideal: there is nothing
worse than the acts that the witch is imagined to perpetrate,
so that the witch's conduct is strictly the opposite of the
ideal. This gives us our first factor in the complex, namely,
the relation of conceptual opposition.

I need not say much about this, for after Hertz a great
deal has been written about polarities, complementaries,
and syzygies in dual symbolic classification, especially with
regard to the sets of opposed values signaled by right and
left. It is important, however, not merely to isolate the re-

lation of opposition from the moral definition of the witch, but also to stress that this relation has a fundamental character that makes it apt to the purpose of relegating the witch to the point of extreme censure. In other words, people resort to opposition as the simplest and most efficacious means of classification. They do so in innumerable institutions and contexts, including moiety systems and symmetric alliance and Manichean theologies, and witchcraft is merely one example of this proclivity.

I mentioned just now that opposite values may be signaled by the opposition of right and left. This spatial expression of nonspatial values, including moral qualities, has an analogue in a second component of the image of the witch. The behavior of the witch is commonly described as inverted, or the witch is said to embody inverted values. This is not simply a metaphor (like "opposite," for that matter), but is frequently a description of the witch's physical posture: the witch proceeds upside down, walking on his hands as the Kaguru imagine, or presents himself backwards. This imaginary inversion makes an apt picture of the perverse nature of the witch, and in itself it is both comprehensible and telling; but once again what we encounter in this component also is simply one example of the operation of a primary factor. When the Lugbara advert to the alien nature of their neighbors, members of other tribes just over the horizon, they say that the latter normally go about upside down. (It is only when you look at them that instantaneously they turn the right way up.) The Lugbara are not saying that all strange peoples are witches: they are expressing the strangeness by resorting to the image of inversion. This is in fact a very common symbolic means of marking a boundary. Similarly, many peoples imagine the world of the dead as the opposite of this, in that the spirits there speak backwards or place opposite values on things; and the Batak say also that the dead climb house-steps downwards, head first, that is, upside down. They are not saying that the spirits of the departed are witches: they are expressing the spirituality of ghosts, in opposition to terrestrial natures, by resorting to the image of inversion. The symbolic operation is the exploitation of the imaginative recourse. Inversion is an elementary mode of marking a contrast — especially at a moral or temporal boundary — and the wide extent to which it is employed, in many customs and ideologies, indicates that it is not merely a formal possibility that is available to the imagination, but that it is a positive proclivity by which men tend to be influenced in their collective representations.

Next, witches habitually go about their business at night. This looks obvious enough, for they work secretly and wish to avoid the gaze of decent people, including that of their victims. An Apache raiding party also used to travel at night, in order to gain the advantage of surprise; and burglars are supposed to operate at night in order not to be seen, either by their victims or by potential witnesses for the prosecution. But of course there is more to the witch's association with night than a practical precaution, especially since it is doubtful that anyone does travel as a witch at night anyway. What we are dealing with is a symbolic, I dare say universal, image by which light and the absence or deprivation of light stand for opposed values and properties of innumerable kinds. The Bible is full of examples of the precellence of light and the opposite condition of darkness; mystical ideology continually resorts to the contrast; and it is a rich source of metaphor in estimating clarity of understanding and moral inclinations. As for the specific connection of witches with night, this too has analogues in other institutions. The first to come to mind is shamanism, in which it is a standard feature that the shaman holds his seance either at night or in a darkened enclosure. This is no doubt because the proceedings have to do with hidden things, with the mystical. (Recall that this word comes from the Greek *mūein*, "to close the eyes.") There is no implication that a shaman is a nefarious person, acting at night in order to conceal his iniquity. Nor of course do I imply that the mystical is symbolized only by darkness, for under some aspects it is enacted in the full radiance of bright light. But the image of the witch combines both the fearsome presence of the powers of darkness and the nocturnal setting of spiritual activity.

This is sometimes symbolized by the color that is appropriate to night, namely, black. European witches used to smear themselves with soot, and witches in other cultures are on occasion distinguished by black appurtenances. In this case again, though, it is not witches alone that are symbolized by black. Our own priests wear black, so does the Mugwe of the Meru, and so also does a Gurung medium. In each instance the color, like night, stands for the mystical character of the status or the undertaking. There is no implication that all persons whose offices are symbolized by black share the horrible attributes of a witch. What particular attributes may be shared, beyond the mystical connection, is a contingent matter of local ideology. The imaginative constant is the resort to color in order to convey the significance. This general feature is nicely glossed by the example of the Kaguru witch: naturally black of skin, he is supposed to cover himself with white ashes, thus employing symbolic color in an image that is opposite to normal human appearance. So the generic factor is color, we may say, while the specific mystical significance is predominantly but not always conveyed by the color of darkness.

The association of a witch with night is reinforced by the usual character of the witch's animal familiar, or of the creature into which the witch can transform himself. Some of the species are the black cat in Europe, the polecat in North America, the fox in Japan, the maned wolf in Brazil, the owl in India, the hyena in East Africa, the bat in the Congo. The obvious and well-recognized attribute that they share is that they are all nocturnal. Some moreover are predators, others carrion-eaters, and yet others are menaces in the dark. These attributes are easy enough to grasp as being appropriate to the nocturnal operation and the dark character of the witch. But once more this is not a singular kind of symbolism that distinguishes only the witch. The individual species are indeed particularly apposite to the image of the witch, but the fact that the status is symbolized by animals is not. The classical demonstration of this fact in anthropology is totemism, in which the classification of men into social groups is symbolized by a parallel classification of animal species. In totemism, a clan may even be associated with a nocturnal species, but there is no usual implication that the social group is composed of witches or that its members have the character of witches. What is happening in this institution is that in discriminating social statuses the members of totemic societies are resorting, by virtue of their tradition, to an extremely common method of symbolism. Ready examples are the animal supporters, such as the lion and the unicorn, in European heraldry; the animal "vehicles," such as the bull of Shiva, that help to identify Hindu deities; the animal-headed gods of Egypt; the birds and other species that represent nations or the states of the U.S.A.; the nicknames and emblems of military formations and sports teams; the terms of moral appraisal that ascribe the strengths and failings of animals to human beings. In all these cases, and in a great many other institutions and figures of speech, men are resorting to a mode of symbolism that has little to do with the particular social facts and a great deal to do with a natural imaginative impulsion. The animal familiar of the witch is merely one instance of the operation of this factor.

Another prominent component in the complex image that we are examining is that very often the witch is supposed to have the power of flight. There is one apparent reason for this, namely, that the action of the witch is usually considered to take place over some distance, either very rapidly or almost instantaneously, and in any case at such a range as could not be covered in the time by a normal human being. The attribute of flight is a simple way to imagine the witch at his swift work, and it is reinforced by those familiars, such as owls and bats, that as natural species are themselves actually capable of flying. That speed is a contributory feature is indicated by the example of the Kalapalo, who explain the rapidity with which a man travels (at night, incidentally) by stating that he came like a maned wolf, the creature that is associated with their witches.

We can conjecture also a negative basis to the employment of the image of flight. When we conceive the operation of some force at a distance, we have the scientific knowledge to enable us to think of a wavelike action, as in the form of a radio beam or a laser or a death ray. But in what terms could we represent such an action, on the part of a witch, if we had not this idiom of physics to rely on? The mystical task, let us consider, is to bring the malign power of one individual to bear, rapidly and over a distance, on another. Lacking the concept of wavelike force, we shall I think find ourselves conceiving that the witch comes directly into contact with his victim; and an immediate recourse is to imagine, with the inspiration of observing airborne species, that the witch flies. Sometimes this action is represented as a detached head (in certain cases with entrails hanging from it) flying through the air; examples come from as far afield as Borneo and Chile. But this image reminds us of Dürer's angels, who appear as cherubic heads equipped with wings, and these lead to a far more general significance in the imagined power of flight. It is a worldwide notion that persons of supernormal status are capable of flight: not only gods and angels and other spirits, but also men who are associated with them or who draw upon their powers; so that saints and shamans and yogis are all credited with mystical flight and sometimes (in Christian tradition, for instance) with physical levitation. Hocart has suggested furthermore that the common practice of carrying kings and other potentates so that they are never in contact with the earth is a ceremonial surrogate for the imagined gift of flight. Once more therefore we have to conclude that a prominent and universal component in the image of the witch has nothing exclusively to do with witches, but is merely one instance of a widely exploited recourse of the imagination in representing persons who possess abnormal powers.

Lastly, let me just mention one more component. I need only mention it, since it is too naturalistic a matter to be very interesting. This is the feature that a witch is supposed to emit a fiery trail or glow as he travels through the air. I am afraid all this means is that marsh gas and similar nocturnal illuminations are very commonly found in the world, and that peoples who imagine witches to fly at night are highly likely to associate their trajectories with the passage of these eerie lights. If the Trobrianders hold that the glow is emitted from the witch's anus, this is just a dramatic touch added to the natural observation. Nevertheless, the component of the aerial light is a very common feature in the image of the witch, and it does reinforce the component of flight. It may not be symbolically so informative as other features, but it is still a contribution to the complex image of the witch. In some cases, moreover, it is a manifestation of fire, and we need no reminder of the fundamental importance everywhere of this lively symbol.

So much, and by necessity rather superficially, for certain factors that characteristically constitute the image: opposition, inversion, darkness, color, animals, flight, and nocturnal lights. I am not asserting that these features alone compose the image, or that all of them must be present, or that witches are necessarily represented by this image. The notion that I am putting forward is in fact doubly polythetic: first, in that disparate phenomena are grouped together under any one factor; second, that the disparate factors are variously and sporadically combined into the image of the witch.

In the first lecture I stressed that the primary factors are heterogeneous and that they are independent of the will. We now see these attributes manifested with special force in the synthetic image of the witch. The operative factors include the relational abstraction of opposition, the spatial metaphor of inversion, and a variety of observable phenomena of nature. The complex that they form has a global distribution and constancy that make it out of the question that each instance should be the result of individual or even traditional invention. As a collective representation, the complex is autonomous, and men have merely altered its particulars according to their circumstances — according to whether they themselves had white or black skins, or whether they had hyenas or the Japanese fox in their environment. It is as though the complex in itself, and not only the several factors out of which it is synthesized, were also primary.

The factors constitute a steady image of the witch, but they are also to be found in the constitution of other images and institutions. For example, the relations and phenomena that we have just surveyed can be combined, with different semantic values according to the appositeness of the materials, into the image of a saint or a shaman. If mystical action at a distance is taken to be definitive, then this too is found in blessing and prayer and spiritual healing. So it is as though men have at their disposal, innately, a limited repertory of imaginative resources, and these, the primary factors, are differentially synthesized into distinct complexes representing disparate social concerns. The factors accrete to the concern, and their meaning in combination corresponds to the concern.

In the case of witchcraft, how are we to account for the synthesis, that is, for the fact that certain primary factors characteristically combine into a recognizable and comprehensible image? I am not at all sure that in principle we can hope to do so. We may in one case or another be able to see how it is that one feature or another is present or has a certain value (white ashes instead of black soot, incest instead of cannibalism), but these diacritical variations are only secondary to the process of synthesis. Even where there is a naturalistic or demonstrable ground to the presence of a particular feature, still we cannot give this a causal expression, and the local explanation does not explain the synthesis. For example, if we assume that there is a patent similarity between the idea of a flying witch and the observation of a will-o'-the-wisp, the phenomenon does not explain the idea, since the idea exists where there is no marsh gas; and the adventitious occurrence of the nocturnal glow, apposite though it may be, does nothing to explain the polythetic synthesis with other factors.

Similar conclusions follow even when a causal connection can be shown to be possible between a feature of the image and some material agent. For example, it has been known for decades that European witches used an ointment containing certain chemical substances, and that they rubbed this into their bodies, apparently into the vaginal membranes and the legs, through which the substances could have entered the blood stream. These substances included hemlock, henbane, belladonna, and aconite, drugs which could conduce to hallucinations, including the sensation of flight. But this does not explain why witches are imagined to fly in societies that do not employ the drugs. Where the image is supported by drug-induced hallucinations, it does not explain the synthesis of the other factors that make up the total image. And in any case the hallucinations do not in themselves explain the factor of flight as an attribute of spirits and saints, shamans and heroes.

If we say then merely that the primary factors accrete around a social concern, what is the concern that underlies the image of the witch? It is articulated as a fear of other men, who can do evil by secret and invisible means. Certainly men have given one another ample occasion to fear other men, but this does not explain the complexity of the image of the witch or its characteristic components. Men everywhere are disposed to fear some other men, yet they adopt many ways apart from the institution of witchcraft in expressing their apprehension and in taking precautions against its object. Actually, it may not be right to say that the factors accrete around the concern, as though the concern came first and the image afterwards. All we know empirically is that the concern, in the form of a conventional unease about certain categories of persons, and the image, as a complex construction of the imagination given also in part by tradition, are found together. The true force of the metaphor of accretion is perhaps that the stated concern, namely, about malign mystical action at a distance, is the most constant definitive feature of the institution and also the theme that imparts a fit meaning to such features as trailing intestines or the invisible draining of the strength of the victims.

Moreover, to concentrate on the social concern, which people are conscious of and can express, leads to the view that witchcraft is a cognitive institution. The burden of my argument however has been that witchcraft is a complex product of the imagination and that it provides evidence of certain proclivities of the imagination. Certainly the institution has a cognitive aspect, for men reflect on their experience and they explain certain untoward events by witchcraft, but the form of the experience and the interpretation of the events are not the results of independent deliberation. If there is a "reality" to the idea of witchcraft, it is to be sought in the grounds and occasions of the image of the witch. Since the components of the image can be seen as products of factors that compose other complex images, the problematical focus is the process of synthesis that combines the components into the characteristic image. This process is not necessarily a response to experience, and we may not presume that it is otherwise determined by social facts. The synthesis may be, as I have suggested earlier, just as "primary" as are the factors that it integrates. In other words, the image of the witch is autonomous and can be conceived as an archetype of the unconscious imagination.

The concept of an archetype, in the sense of a primordial mental image, has suffered from obscurity and also from obscurantism, and it has fallen into discredit in the eyes of those for whom for whom the work of Jung is not entirely creditable. In adverting to this concept, however, I am not trying to darken or diminish understanding but to advance analysis; and in formulating the results of comparative study by means of the word *archetype* I am not subscribing to Jung's psychology as a system. In undertaking the present investigation, I was not committed in advance to a Jungian view of the unconscious. My question was, How is social anthropology possible? The outcome, so far as the institution of witchcraft is concerned, is the notion of a psychic constant in the form of an autonomous image to which the human mind is naturally predisposed. *Archetype* happens to be the right word to denote this complex product of the unconscious.

There is in particular a distinction of method to be made. Typically, I take it, Jung's ideas on archetypes were derived from correspondences between images in the dreams or fantasies of patients and in alchemical manuscripts and hermeneutic sources. For the social anthropologist, on the other hand, the major sources are the reports of world ethnography, an incomparably vaster field of evidence and one that the comparativist nevertheless manages to comprehend as the widest testimony to the collective forms of human experience. As for the present investigation, moreover, there is a marked contrast between Jung's studies and the approach that I have outlined. I think I am right in saying that Jung's analyses of what he regarded as archetypes were not only culturally limited but were also highly particularistic, and even idiosyncratic, in that each archetype was interpreted in terms of its own proper significance. My own method, though, has been to investigate the archetype of the witch by analysis into primary factors that are not exclusively associated with witchcraft. If I have on occasion referred to the products of these factors (particular colors, sides, sounds, textures) as semantic units, this was with the explicit gloss that the units could carry variable and even opposite meanings from one cultural context to another. In postulating a repertory of primary factors, I have presented a possibility that so far as I know Jung was not concerned with; and by concentrating on the principles of synthesis that constitute primary factors into archetypes and that discriminate one archetype from another, I have taken what appears to be a quite different direction of research.

Nevertheless, both of these approaches to the topic of archetypes are exercises in depth psychology. If the evidence of the social anthropologist consists in the first place of social facts and collective representations, this affords him only an advantage; for as social facts these representations have a relative autonomy, a generality, and a coercive force that objectify them for the purposes of analysis and comparison. Durkheim was quite right, I think, in propounding the notion of an entirely formal pyschology that would be a sort of common ground for individual psychology and for sociology, and in suggesting that the comparative study of collective representations might seek the "laws of collective ideation" or of "social mentality" in general. This enterprise would lead, hypothetically, to the establishment of propositions that were valid equally for the individual and for the collective, with an exclusive substantive locus in neither.

The essential, if we are to say anything fundamental about human nature, is to find the common term of individual and collective. I have spoken here as though "the imagination" were in effect such a common term; and in analyzing the image of the witch I have alluded to properties that can be common both to individual consciousnesses and to collective representations. But these properties are such as, empirically, must inhere in some locus or entity or system of phenomena that is common to both types of manifestation of the imagination. According to received ideas, which I have no reason to question in this instance, this can reside only in the human organism; and the plainest and most economical inference is that this means the brain. The present state of knowledge concerning this organ, the most complicated natural system known, is, I gather, still relatively superficial and partial; and I am not relying on neurophysiology when I say that I interpret the primary factors and the modes of synthesis as spontaneous manifestations of properties of the brain. The strength of this accommodating hypothesis is that it accounts for the global distribution of the characteristic image of the witch, and at the same time

for the constancy of the factors as apparently innate predispositions. It is on these premises that I find it convenient
to regard the archetypes as vectors of consciousness. There
is nothing in principle that is particularly difficult to accept in this metaphor. All it necessarily implies, in the first
place, is that the brain responds to percepts differentially;
for instance, that it responds especially to red rather than
to other hues, or to percussion as distinct from more mel-
lifluous sounds. There is some experimental support for this
assumption, in addition to the weight of ethnographic indications. In some cases, in connection with certain primary
factors or archetypes (such as percussion, the half man), it is
moreover possible to suggest empirical grounds for their
presence or their prominence.

Among the heterogeneous primary factors there falls a
line that divides them into two types: those that are abstract (such as the relation of binary opposition) and those
that are perceptual (such as color, texture). There is an in-
viting correspondence here with the contrasted functions
of the cerebral hemispheres. It is tempting to link the
respective factors causally to these functions: the abstract
factors to the left hemisphere, the perceptual ones to the
right. A plausible hypothesis is that the comparatively restricted number of abstract factors has to do with the analytical function of the left hemisphere, and the more extensive
range of the perceptual factors with the function of the
right. A conceivable process is that these contrasted cerebral
functions combine in an imaginative tropism, a synthetic
response to natural foci of attraction among phenomena,
whether social or physical, and that the product is the
archetype.

With these considerations we are far beyond the present

limits of proof, but I am not suggesting that it is essential to fall in with speculations of this kind in order to assent to to the method that I have proposed. I suggest only that the dichotomy among the primary factors, and their synthesis into the archetype, are consistent with current opinion about the lateral functions of the brain; and that this ultimate locus is consistent with the unconscious generation of the archetypes and with the likelihood that these complex images are the products of genetically inherited predispositions.

What may lie at a deeper level of probing into the imaginative operations of the brain, in the form of neuroelectrical events, is a tantalizing sequel among further questions that propose themselves, if hardly one that a comparativist can have an opinion about. I mention it, however, in order to put us on our guard against inappropriate preconceptions when, as is almost inevitable, we do speculate on the cerebral grounds to collective representations. I am alluding to Wittgenstein's salutary comments:

No supposition seems to me more natural than that there is no process in the brain correlated with associating or with thinking; so that it would be impossible to read off thought-processes from brain-processes. I mean this: if I talk or write there is, I assume, a system of impulses going out from my brain and correlated with my spoken or written thoughts. But why should the *system* continue further in the direction of the centre? . . . It is . . . perfectly possible that certain psychological phenomena cannot be investigated physiologically, because physiologically nothing corresponds to them.

For the more ascertainable present, let me conclude this lecture by resuming some of the main points. We have

moved from the sociology of mystical crime, by way of in-
duction from the global comparison of social facts, to certain
apparent properties of the human brain. These properties
are seen as determinants in the constitution of collective
representations, not only of witchcraft but in effect universally and with regard to numerous other institutions. As
such, they act as initial limits to the imagination, rather as
do certain logical constraints on the forms of discursive reasoning. This conclusion runs contrary to the received idea of
romantic individualism that, however constrained we may
be by the dictates of society and the puny capacities of the
human organism, we have an unfettered liberty in the exercise of the imagination. At the level of collective representations, our investigation of the image of the witch tends to
reduce the scope and assurance of this comfortable assumption.

Evasive Fantasies

THE WORD *imagination* has among its meanings, in addition to that of the relatively passive formation of images, the idea of active contrivance, inventing, devising. In our first lecture I sketched some of the proclivities and constraints that influence the imagination through collective representations; in the second, I examined a prominent example of a synthetic image to which men appear to be naturally predisposed; and in the present and final lecture I want to consider a contrasted inclination that is equally characteristic of the contrivances of the imagination.

My case so far has been directed against intellectualism: not, that is, against thought or analysis or any other rational deployment of the intellect, but against the presumption that in the study of social facts, and more generally in the interpretation of human experience, intellectual considerations must be preponderant or even decisive.

A familiar instance of this prejudice is to be found in recent views on totemism. This protean institution is claimed to be an illustration of certain modes of thought; in effect, a form of classification. The right interpretation of totemism is asserted to pertain to the understanding; the demands to which it responds, and the way in which it tries to meet them, are, it is contended, primarily of an intellectual kind. To the extent that the terms of the hypothesis are clear, this is not anything like a good argument. To begin with, it is to some extent truistic, in that the institution is defined in advance as a classification of natural phenomena (animal species, and so on) which in some circumstances is employed as an ancillary classification of human beings. This correlation of categories permits a number of different analyses, and at the limit the analysis of a particular instance of totemism is a contextual interpretation of the contingent social facts that compose it at a certain place and period. But the characteristic feature is the intimate association that is made between natural species and persons, and this precisely is left unexplained by the intellectualist hypothesis. There is indeed an aphoristic aside to the effect that natural species are resorted to in this form of classification because they are "good to think," but this begs the question. We cannot know that totemic peoples rationally constructed their schemes of association, and so far as I am aware we have no good evidence that they cogitate or otherwise act intellectually (that is, "think") by means of the distinctions and correlations of their totemic categories.

There is also the plain objection that, so far as the organization of social life is concerned, the totemic classification offers in a crucial respect a very bad pattern of inference. Natural species are strictly endogamous, mating each only with its own kind: white cockatoos with white cockatoos, and so on. But if human beings are White Cockatoos, it is precisely and primarily with other White Cockatoos that they absolutely may not marry. So if descent groups are discriminated as natural species in order, as has been maintained, to regulate marital exchanges, their members can be

rationally guided by their totemic affiliations only by avoid-
ing the very inference to which they are invited by the relations among the species. Intellectually speaking, that is,
from a logical point of view, this is perverse, and it cannot
be the point of totemism.

Actually, I doubt that any anthropologist who has taken
the matter seriously, that is, in the interpretation of ethnographic details, has been persuaded that totemism is at all
to be accounted for in such terms, so it is a question why an
interpretation of the kind should have exercised much sway.
Partly because of expository rhetoric, no doubt, but there is
a more serious reason that answers to my present concerns.
Theories about totemism are made up by academics, and the
business of the academic is to bring intellect to bear on phenomena. We are, in a word, intellectuals; and intellectualism is our right and proper commitment. It is because of this
background, I take it, that topics such as rationality and
structures of thought and species that are good to think have
such a vogue; also, paradoxically, that they are sometimes
treated with less intellectual rigor than they demand. Yet,
as comparativists especially, we are supposed to come to
terms, as nearly as we can, with the intrinsic properties of
social facts; and a doctrinaire intellectualism, even when it
is not tendentious, can powerfully prevent us doing this.

Now we have already glanced at totemism, in the second
lecture, and the object in that place was to show that witchcraft and totemism were together merely two instances, out
of a great many, of a natural imaginative impulsion to sym-
bolize social statuses and attributes by resort to animal species. Against that setting, it seems to me sounder, and more
in accord with the characteristic features of totemism, simply to acknowledge that animals are good to imagine. What

people will then think, or whether they will think at all, with these imaginative resources, is a highly contingent matter, and I rather doubt that we can infer or predict much about it. The proclivity is the thing, and once we have identified it in a satisfactory range of social facts there may be nothing more than we can usefully do about it — except to be that much better prepared to recognize it in the constitution of further institutions.

After that much preamble, I now want to pursue the argument in a different direction. Instead of examining, as in the second lecture, a synthetic image that is naturally presented to men and spontaneously represented by them to the ethnographer, I shall take up a type of social fact that is generally not discriminated by its bearers but is instead largely a product of the anthropologist's categories. This is the topic of myth — and if you are dismayed at the prospect of hearing yet more on this battered subject, I can hardly blame you. But I think the approach that I have adopted so far can place even myth under a new aspect. The outcome will not be entirely new, of course, and in part I shall in fact be asking you to recognize more clearly what you already know, just as I did with the image of the witch. Here again it is the change of aspect, in the first place, that is important; then the implications that we can derive from it concerning the properties of human nature.

As in the case of the witch, difficulty begins with definition. I need not bore you with a rehearsal of the numerous meanings that have been given to the word *myth* by anthropologists. The essential is that none is indisputably apt and that there is no precise definition generally adopted in anthropology. Nor therefore is there a clear line to be drawn between a myth and a legend, folktale, fairy story, or some other kind of traditional narrative. As for the conditions in which a myth is narrated: it may be secret or public; it may be accompanied by a rite or by none; it may be recited in a set and word-perfect order, or it may be elaborated into many variations; it may be thought to have certain effects, or it may be received just as a diverting tale; and so on through a variety of settings and conditions not worth the time to list.

Much the same is the case with theories of myth: that myth reflects history, provides a social charter, responds to natural phenomena, expresses perennial human concerns, embodies a metaphysics, reaffirms eternal verities, copes with historical change, and so on almost endlessly. Often enough the anthropologist is able to demonstrate a concordance between a myth and something or other in the society to which it belongs, which to some extent is only to be expected; but the temptation is then to extend the local interpretation into a theory that will apply to myth in general, and this stretch of ambition has not met with so general a success.

One version that has made a special stir is that of structural analysis, with the specific aim of isolating fundamental structures of the human mind. In this the vocabulary of analysis typically includes terms such as *opposition, transformation, homology, transposition,* and so on. The formalization is no doubt good method, even if Andrew Lang would have been unlikely to find anything surprising in the narrative devices to which the terms correspond, but it is the inspiration behind this quasi-logical style of analysis that I want to stress. The idea in question is that myth works progressively toward the resolution of contradictions: in other words, that myth is not only an intellectual construction but also a discursive instrument of logic. This is a striking approach, but it has not, I think I am right in saying, procured full conviction by its results. Even if we accept for the while a pretty lax use of formal terms, entertain the intellectualist premises, and leave aside the numerous myths to which the theory patently does not apply, there is still considerable difficulty about the particular cases that are presented for analysis. The contradictions in question can often be seen as such only from a point of view that is not known to be shared by the possessors of the myth, and it can be hard to see why the latter should be worried by them even if they did conceive them as contradictions. In any case, it has been well observed by one critic that structural analysis of this kind extracts from myth not only a different but a lesser meaning. In a number of analyses, also, it must be said, the method has been subverted by an unsatisfactory understanding and treatment of the ethnographic sources. Such failures do not invalidate the method in the abstract, as a hypothetical ideal in the service of an ultimate theory; but all the same it would be more impressive if the aims of this highly intellectualist style of analysis were more convincingly carried into effect.

Now I am not arguing against structural analysis, and certainly not against the ambition to determine fundamental properties (whether they are "structures" is another matter) of the human mind. My point for the moment is to contend that there is no satisfactory theory of myth, and that the failure of anthropology is the most marked in the most determinedly intellectualist endeavor to construct one. A chief reason for this state of affairs is, I think, that the word *myth* does not denote, except factitiously, a discrete class of phenomena. It is to a high degree what Wittgenstein called an "odd-job" word, and in that case we can hardly expect it to form the subject of consistent theoretical propositions. It has indeed its ordinary use in a syllabus, where it makes a rough discrimination of certain matters from topics such as kinship (another odd-job word, if ever there was one), economics, or politics; it has a similar use in the organization of an ethnographic monograph; and when we make a contextual interpretation of a "myth" it need not occasion any confusion of thought. In each instance the word may have an entirely convenient use, but the variety of anthropological connotations is far from laying even the grounds for a theory of myth.

Yet on the other hand there is undeniably a quality that we do respond to in certain "mythical" narratives, abundantly reported from around the world from New Zealand to Tierra del Fuego, that appear to bear family resemblances one to another despite the greatest geographical distances and cultural disparities. Perhaps it is feasible to make something of these apparently qualitative resemblances. Let us see if we can get anywhere by trying to isolate certain characteristic features from the kind of narrative that we commonly recognize as myth. Only let us at the same time keep in mind a methodological caution: it is the features that we are interested in, not the definition of a type of narrative in which they are presumed to inhere. Accordingly, we shall not be concerned to claim that the features are characteristic of myth alone, or that a narrative must possess such features if it is to count as a myth. Not only a premature typology of myth, but the very intention to construct any topology at all, has repeatedly frustrated attempts to formulate comparative propositions. We are not after types, but properties. If we can isolate significant features, then we shall try to see what they are properties of.

The key was provided in 1903 by Durkheim and Mauss, who wrote that metamorphoses, the transmission of qualities, the substitution of persons, souls, and bodies, beliefs about the materialization of spirits and the spiritualization of material objects, were the elements of folklore. This is certainly a very striking feature: Zeus perpetually changes form, and so often do mythical heroes; a frog changes into a prince; words change into diamonds and snakes. There are myriad examples of this feature, this inconstancy of form, and it is so common that perhaps we should be surprised if any corpus of tales from an exotic culture failed to include instances of it. We take it pretty much for granted, and yet it contradicts the premise of constancy on which we base our dealings with other individuals and our manipulations of the nonhuman world. By and large, people and things remain much the same over considerable periods of time: they do not commonly change in form under our eyes, and this invariancy permits us to make predictions about them and to guide our behavior accordingly. In many narratives, however, metamorphosis is as reliable a feature as is conservation of form in our practical lives. We are indeed accustomed to this mythical quality, but it is not to be taken for granted. Nor, as we at once see, is it peculiar to a strictly defined class of myths: it is found just as characteristically in what we ordinarily distinguish as legends and fairy stories, and in other tales from Ovid to Kafka; while conversely it is quite often not found in some of the powerful narratives (that of Oedipus is one example) that we have no hesitation in singling out as myths.

We can conceive metamorphosis either as a positive capacity or else negatively, as an abrogation of constraint. If we adopt the latter view, for the present at any rate, it becomes easier to appreciate that the inconstancy of form is only one of a number of modes in which certain narratives represent the evasion of constraints. The main respects in which this is done are time and space: it is a characteristic feature that the protagonist can transport himself effortlessly and instantaneously from one point to another, either in the development of the action or in his physical setting. Often the narrative proceeds without making the transition overtly, yet placing the protagonist suddenly and inexplicably in a different time or season or at another place. These are events that are so thoroughly familiar that I need not labor the point. The matter on which I should like to focus your interest is that in respect of time and space, which in real life impose ineluctable constraints, mythical and other narratives assume the possibility of an untrammeled freedom of state. This much is easily enough conceded, yet at the same time so easily that it is odd to find Jan van Baal having to ask, only very recently, what is the obviously consequential question: "Why do students of myth pay so little attention to its most challenging characteristic, the fact that every myth confronts us with at least one event or situation which is physically or humanly impossible?"

Well, that really is the question, but before we conjecture an answer there is a realization that I need to urge on you. The abrogation of constraint—in form, space, time, personality, logic, and incidental attributes—is not simply a characteristic feature of the narratives. It is a characteristic feature of our imaginations that we should so unhesitatingly entertain, concede, and be convinced by impossibilities of these kinds when certain narratives present them to us. In this regard we share that frame of mind, presumably, with those who, individually or by the accu-

mulation of cultural inheritance, were responsible for the
presence of such features in the narratives that for us are objects of study. Fabricators, audiences, and analysts are
bound together by common criteria of fantasy and by common imaginative predispositions.

The field of evidence in responding to van Baal's question
is not limited to one discrete type of narrative or to any particular ethnographical source of mythical materials: it is human imagination, without regard to discipline or to social
context. In these respects we are at a plane of generality
such as was the basis for our investigation into the image of
the witch. The great difference however is that in that case
we were confronted with a clear and positive construction;
whereas in the present case there is no such complex but instead a set of features, negatively defined, that dissolve images and permit an infinity of phenomenal conjunctions. The
image of the witch condenses primary factors; the characteristic features in myth disperse the images in an unbounded
evasive fantasy.

If we keep in mind our precept that the property is the
thing, the next step is to seek it in phenomena other than
myth, and the obvious institutions to look at are other forms
of discursive art. For a number of literate and sophisticated
civilizations the first is fiction. Here there is surely a characteristic abrogation of constraint, in that the immediate effect
of fictional narratives — when well done, naturally — is
that of a release from intention and from the deliberate exercise of rational appraisal. This is not merely an example
of the conditions of aesthetic pleasure, nor again is it only
the result of an evocative literary skill: it is a response to a
form of art that, to varying degrees, exploits the inconstancies and the rapid transitions that are characteristic in myth.

Only just as we do not say that all myths have these features, so we need not expect that all fictional narratives shall have them either. It is enough that the narrator shall on occasion transport us from one location to another, or from one period to some other time, or even place us as quasi observers simultaneously in different places and times or in the personalities of different characters. The sequence of events can be chronologically disordered, or the accomplishment of reported acts can be placed radically in doubt, and in many other ways the fiction can quite persuade us in regards that ordinarily speaking we should know to be physically or logically impossible. We have no difficulty in accommodating ourselves to such breaches of normal constraints. On the contrary, we seek them out, and probably in part specifically for the sake of this recalcitrant inconstancy. Hence the significant phrase in one of Lévy-Bruhl's notebooks in which he writes of the sense of "luxury" with which we abandon ourselves to fictions and are no longer subjected to the demands of reason.

Much the same can be said of staged forms of art, such as plays, opera, and ballet, only in one respect more remarkably. When we read a fictional narrative the words provide occasions for the inner construction of images; whereas what we see on the stage is externally acted out for us, and our imaginative responses have to start from given forms of perception. Nevertheless, the abrogations of constraints, against the normal run of reality, do not lose their power to captivate. This becomes plainer in proportion as the type of art is governed by stagey conventions, and most of all perhaps in ballet. The conventions have to be learned and tacitly accepted, and even then a great deal is left to the imaginative participation of the spectator in following what is compre-

hensible (if that is the right word) only by an imaginative
suspension of rational assessment. My own favorite example
happens to be *Petrouchka*, but the features in question can be
discerned in numerous other presentations of dramatic art.

The allusions to drama lead plainly enough to ritual. Here
too we find the constraints of reality constantly flouted in
the name of spiritual personages and mystical connections of
cause and effect. Substances are transformed, objects are
spiritualized, gestures act immaterially to produce unseen
changes. In blessing and cursing, neither time nor distance
need be a barrier to what is intended. Officiants change
character for the while and assume powers that in ordinary
life cannot be their own. This is especially true of the rites
of shamanism, in which the medium may be possessed by
other personalities or turn into creatures of other species or
fly to other places and to the otherworld. We need not
bother with the question whether participants or observers
are convinced that these things actually happen: they are
imagined to happen, under the sway of collective representations, and for my present purpose that is enough.

Just as in the second lecture we found an imaginative analogue to the witch in the figure of the shaman, so now we
can interpret the public powers of the shaman as having
their analogue, conversely, in the secret powers that are attributed to the witch. The difference in this perspective is
that we have seen the shaman as exercising powers — specifically, powers inconsistent with ordinary circumstances
— of an open and socially approved kind such as are appropriate to ritual; whereas the supposed abilities of the
witch are maleficent and are conventionally at least the objects of fear and distrust. So the important common feature
between shaman and witch has nothing to do with the se-

mantic or emotional content of the representations. What counts, for the purpose of the present comparison, is the property of immunity from certain material and conceptual constraints. The immoderate capacities that in myth are attributed to protagonists are acted out dramatically by the shaman, and are imagined to be exercised in dark concealment by the witch.

As a last institutional example of the property in question there is the great religious leader. Typically, the spiritual master possesses to an impressive extent the power of transcending the limits of ordinary possibility such as we have traced from myth through a rapid survey of institutions of very disparate kinds. A prominent manifestation of this mythical liberty is to be found of course in the performance of miracles, including the ultimate feat of immunity from the necessity to die. Thus the master may defy his judge at a public trial with the claim that he cannot be killed since he is not mortal; pass from the midst of spectators by inexplicable means; reappear in an instant at a great distance to the astonishment of his followers, who will not accept that he is alive until they have touched his body. The example I have just cited is that of Apollonius escaping from the clutches of a Roman emperor and translating himself (like a shaman or a witch) into the presence of a doubting Demetrius; but it is typical of other mystical personages, and it is probably not the only such case that you can think of.

I hope you will not have been bored by this short survey of familiar matters, for it is instructive that the examples shall in fact be thoroughly familiar to you. And of course it would be easy to extend the list of comparable social facts by adding magicians, prophets, saints, even political and military leaders, and other personages who on occasion can all be distinctively credited with the immunity from ordinary constraint that is a characteristic feature in myth. What this range of collective representations testifies to is an intrinsic vagrancy of the imagination and a constant impulsion to evade external limitations.

But of course it is not only in collective representations and in social forms that we encounter these testimonies to an important motive in human nature. You will already have made the connection, I am sure, with dreams. In these, with a striking immediacy, we experience directly the gamut of images and operations that we have been examining in institutions: metamorphoses, transpositions, fluctuations in form and qualities, abrupt transitions, immoderate powers (including that of flight), illogicalities, and in general all manner of inconstancy and recalcitrance to constraint. It is something of a commonplace that there are interesting similarities between myths (certain myths, that is) and dreams; and what I want to stress is not merely this comparability but two further points. First, that the similarities in question — that is, with regard to what I began by isolating as characteristic features in myth — are found in addition throughout a wide and heterogeneous range of other social forms. Second, that in contrast with the collective representations, imposed by tradition and occasion, dreams are distinctively individual and spontaneous. Admitted, the greater part of the materials out of which dreams are composed is probably cultural; but some components are so practically universal, as are the operations to which they are subjected, that they cannot be ascribed to the differentiating influences of culture. So what the correspondences between collective and individual testify to, in this comparison, is an aspect of the imagination that is truly intrinsic to human nature. This in turn can be conceived as a normal, if disorderly, function of consciousness.

We may for the moment sum up the outcome of our rapid determination of characteristic features in myth. The features are characteristic not simply of certain myths but of the imagination. This is an aspect of human experience that has generally been ignored or underrated in anthropology; perhaps because of a presumption that it was a fitter subject for introspective psychology or for a phenomenological philosophy, perhaps because it was foreign to intellectualism. There was also perhaps at work the notion that there are set limits to what can be said about this faculty, and that much of what can be said can be stated only in negative terms. However, the ground that we have covered in these lectures tends to show that the imagination can be studied in positive terms, by means of a comparison of collective representations from around the world and in the records of history. This method of study permits the isolation of primary factors, synthetic images, and standard operations. These are not the products of deliberate inventive ingenuity: they are independent of the will, or, in other words, they are properties of the unconscious. This deep level of experience is not entirely dark and inaccessible, as Freud's work on individual psyches led him to think. It can be investigated in empirical terms, through collective representations and social forms, exactly like any social facts in such fields of inquiry as prescriptive alliance or the symbolism of ritual or the maintenance of public order. In certain respects at least the unconscious side of human nature can be investigated in this way because it is, as ethnographic comparison proves, a genuinely collective unconscious. Investigations such as the present lectures can demonstrate —

or could demonstrate, at any rate, if carried out in properly convincing detail — the cogency of Jung's assertion that the original structural components of the psyche are of no less surprising a uniformity than are those of the human body. As for the etiology of this uniformity, which we are in a position to say is worldwide, I shall do no more for the present than conjecture, after Jung, that it is "somehow" connected with the brain.

All of this diverges widely from the intellectualist bent of modern anthropology, with its concern for questions of cognition and rationality. I am not saying that it goes against such interests, for they also are aspects of a complex human nature: they are intrinsically important and analytically fascinating, and I do not in the least propose that they should be set at a discount in favor of a concentration on the imagination. I am urging, rather, that manifestations of the imagination, under its most general and specific aspects, can be recognized and can be studied comparatively as social facts.

As for the method of doing so, I said earlier that there is no special trick to it, and all the inquiry calls for is to follow Durkheim's precept in the *Rules of Sociological Method*: "Take as the object of your research nothing but a group of phenomena defined in advance by certain external characteristics that they have in common, and then include in the research all phenomena that answer to this definition." This is all I have done in these lectures: to isolate certain properties of social facts, initially in given types of institution, and then to trace these properties wherever they can be found and without regard to any kind of typology. The undertaking can be seen as a further exercise in what Waismann described as the quiet and patient undermining of categories over the whole field of thought; and a critical instrument for doing this in anthropology is the concept that social facts may be analyzed into characteristic features in polythetic combination.

Of course, the method does not tell us what phenomena to find interesting or what properties to concentrate on, and I can only hope that the outcome so far has somewhat justified my own interest in what appear to me to be primary factors of human experience. But I realize that the extent to which you are likely to share this commitment will depend in part on what are the implications of the argument.

At the end of the first lecture I made the point that to concede any directive influence means that we are not so free and not so individual as we thought we were; at the end of the second, I concluded that there were certain intrinsic limits to imaginative collective representations; and in the present address I have indicated something of the extent to which we are under the influence of a recalcitrance to constraint, or a positive proclivity to imaginative disorder. These determinants, not being products of the will, tend to show that even in the activity of the imagination, where we might have thought ourselves most in command of our inner lives, we are what we are thanks initially to a nature that is common to our species. While it is a truism that our consciousness is largely a product of our institutions, the conviction that we can legislate for our social forms, and can in principle manipulate them at will, provides some support to romantic individualism. But the more we discover that primary factors and their products act as determinants of the unconscious, the less feasible it is to claim the imaginative liberty that would make us artists of our own forms of consciousness.

The restrictions imposed on that idealistic liberty may not appear very significant in particular instances; but what is decisive is the concession that the influence of any deter-minants of the kind, however conditional or prevenient they may be, can be established. Once this step is taken, and a formative constraint on any aspect of our experience is rec-ognized, we can have no a priori knowledge of the extent to which we may be governed by such factors in ways that at present we do not even suspect.

Since Durkheim met the resistance that I mentioned in the opening lecture, the development of comparative social studies has on the whole had the consequence, I think, of reducing progressively man's sense of his individuality and autonomy. It seems to me probable that a hundred years ago an Englishman or an American (not that in Virginia there was that much difference) could regard himself as more in command of himself, though under more autocratic forms of government, than can an educated person today. The coer-cive force of social facts can be seen increasingly to extend into the construction of reality, modes of thought, con-science, emotions, and now the imagination. There is on the other hand no countertrend in comparativism, so far as I know, that makes an argument against the dominance of in-stitutions; and the more it is conceived that institutions themselves may in some regards be directly dependent on the organization of the brain, the less likely it is that this trend in the assessment of man and his powers will be re-versed.

I have been speaking, you realize, as though the increasing diminution in man's sense of his autonomy was deplorable and to be resisted if possible. It is true that morally that is my inclination, but of course it is quite beside the point.

Our task is to discover by the comparative analysis of social facts what are the bounds of understanding, the range of human powers, and the constituents of consciousness. This is an empirical undertaking, and if a case is made by positive demonstration then the implications are just whatever they happen to be. We may not be able to do anything about them, but we have to come to terms with them if we are to make a right estimation of ourselves.

There is in fact one sequel to be drawn out from the essential vagrancy of the imagination. We might be inclined to think that this characteristic manifested the preponderant function of the right cerebral hemisphere, while the stringency of reason was a product of the other; and that these contrasted mental activities would be complementary and as it were equally proportioned. I am fairly convinced, however, that the more we attend to human discourse, and to the course of our own thought, the less it will appear that this is a correct statement of the matter. We can find the characteristic features of myth in a wide range of other institutions and forms of behavior; but it is hard to see that rationality has anything like the same weight and distribution. This is largely an impressionistic assessment, and the evidences cannot be quantified in the way that the comparison requires, but it is a matter on which defensible judgments can be made. My own observation at any rate leads me to a fairly decided view. Men do not reason often; they do not reason for long at a time; and when they do reason they are not very good at it.

I tend to think moreover that these would be fairly general findings of an accurate examination of everyday communications and, where possible, of the things that run through our heads. As academics we prize reason and we take it to be a dominant activity on the part of Homo sapiens; but we all know at the same time how desperately hard it can be to screw ourselves up to face the necessity of thought, and also how fitfully and inefficiently we usually do it. If the matter is that hard for men whose trade is exact thought, what is the case with other men who are not professionally committed to it? Do they really govern their conduct and their conversations by firm if informal canons of logic and in the light of rational considerations? In general, and so far as these matters can well be estimated, the answer is surely that they (by which I must mean we) do not. Whether we are in the high forests of the interior of Borneo or in an Oxford public house or "The Mousetrap," the discourse that a recording device would normally pick up does not express orderly ratiocination. (I am not talking about the special case of academics, despite what Wittgenstein called the slightly hysterical style of university talk.) If we want a truer impression of the operation of men's minds, as uttered in their everyday communications, we should turn not to ethnographers but to the plays of Chekhov, Samuel Beckett, and Harold Pinter. That this is not more obvious is a consequence, I infer, of the intellectualist bias of anthropology; just as is the concomitant neglect of what is preponderantly characteristic of men, namely, the vagrancy, the inconsequentiality, and the fantasy of their imagination.

You will no doubt have found much in what I have said to be reminiscent of Freud's distinction between the primary and secondary processes, the id and the ego, and there is indeed a similarity. But there are important differences. First, that Freud reached his conclusions from the psychoanalysis of individuals, whereas the present argument rests in the main on the comparative study of collective representations. Second, that for Freud the id was defined as the arena of desires and wishes, whereas the characteristic features that I have isolated are not conative: they can be defined formally, almost as a variable geometry of images, and they have no intrinsic connection with the sexual and destructive impulses that to Freud were so clamorous in the id. It can seem tempting to attribute these conative qualities to the collective modes of the imagination, because there is an oneiric quality to certain myths and mystical institutions. That is, to be more exact, they share with dreams the gamut of metamorphoses, transpositions, and other inconstancies; and, because after Freud we interpret dreams by reference to repressed wishes, it may seem reasonable to analyze the institutions also by reference to otherwise concealed desires. But Freud's interpretation of dreams is only one of the very many that have been contrived over millennia, and it is not self-evidently the best ground on which to analyze materials that despite formal resemblances are not dreams.

For that matter, it may be a more correct position to say that collective representations can provide a surer basis for psychoanalysis than does a particular theory for the interpretation of dreams. Freud once declared to the unseen audience of one of his new introductory lectures on psychoanalysis that they would not expect him to have much that was new to tell them about the id. According to the argument of the present lectures, however, it may turn out that by the comparative analysis of ethnographic materials we can tell a great deal that is new, and in positive terms, about modes of the unconscious imagination that are characteristic of mankind. If the recalcitrance to constraint and the propensity to disordered fantasy are as central as I have made out, then these are natural proclivities of the psyche that are at least comparable in importance with the lusts of the id as clues to our inner nature.

It may be helpful to insist further on the etiological differences between Freud's largely negative account of the primary processes and the comparative generalizations that I have advanced. Methodologically, my ground for doing so is Occam's razor: that entities are not to be multiplied beyond necessity. If we approach the imagination and its modes via collective representations, it appears by contrast that Freud's account calls onto the stage of the unconscious a number of entities that, under the aspect of social facts, have no clear right to be there.

Freud observes that in the manifest content of dreams we very often find pictures and situations recalling familiar themes in fairy tales, legends, and myths; these include the illogicality and the indifference to space and time that we have taken to be characteristic in myth. But Freud then straightway infers that the interpretation of such dreams therefore throws light on "the original interests" that created these themes, so that the work of dream-interpretation will uncover the "raw material" of the myths, and this is often enough sexual. The dream itself is a "pathological product," in a class that includes hysterical symptoms, obsessions, and delusions. It is produced by the "psychical energy" provided by an unconscious impulse in conflict with a resistance, and the cathexis is directed toward the fulfillment of an instinctual wish. The id is indeed filled with energy, and Freud concludes in fact that all there is to the id is "instinctual cathexes seeking discharge." Since the dream is symptomatic of this process, it is hence Freud's

battery of agents that constitute the original interests behind the myths and that elucidate their meaning.

Now I am not in a position to say anything about the
clinical or therapeutic value of Freud's analysis of dreams,
but it does not appear to answer at all well to our investigation into collective representations. The inferential constructs of libidinous interests, pathology, psychical energy,
resistance, and instinctual wishes are either misplaced or
gratuitous when they are applied to social facts. They are
not derived from the social facts but are imputed to them,
and my criticism is that it is neither necessary nor advantageous to do so. We certainly need not, for instance,
ascribe to myths the pathological character that is said to
define dreams; and we cannot demonstrate the character
therapeutically by identifying, in a linguistic tradition, an
analogue to the resistance that in a patient is the motive and
meaning of a dream. In collective representations the dream-
like characteristics appear, by their generality and prepon-
derance, to be entirely normal; and it has been my repeated
contention that we should recognize these characteristics as
natural products of imaginative consciousness. Nor is it even
necessary to introduce the desideratum of meaning: the primary factors furnish semantic units merely in the sense that
they can convey an infinity of meanings, and the inconstancies of the collective imagination can serve innumerable semantic ends. As for the inconstancies themselves, it is a fair
inference that they exhibit a normal operation of the organ
of consciousness, that is, the brain, in a state of inattention
or when it is not focused on a deliberative task. If we consider this familiar aspect of imaginative consciousness as being more or less coterminous with the id, we may even
conclude that we can get a clearer view of the id itself from

the comparison of collective representations than from a Freudian analysis of individual psychopathology.

Allow me next to bring out another implication of the present argument, and this time one that may have more practical consequences. The resemblances between dreams and works of literary imagination have often been noted, and particularly well by Charles Rycroft. One very interesting point he makes is this: "It is not that the poet or writer actively masters the iconography of his times in order to be able to universalize his private emotions, but that one aspect of his 'negative capability' is an exceptional sensitivity and receptivity to the iconographical network that constitutes the culture of his time." In our present context this observation leads to the idea that the comparativist must be exceptionally sensitive to the iconographical, or imaginative, resources that constitute culture in general; and I should like to suppose that the kind of undertaking that I have sketched in these lectures may have something of that effect. If it is right that social anthropology becomes possible to the extent that we identify primary factors and their products, then to extend the repertory of such factors will increase the receptivity of the anthropologist and will facilitate his recognition of the "network" that is composed by any particular culture that he analyzes.

That is straightforward enough. But there is, I think, a concomitant that makes far harder demands and for which there may well be no methodological precepts. If the writer produces his effects by a means shared also by the anthropologist, so conversely does the anthropologist depend for the conveyance of his understanding on the literary skill of the writer. This is not a logical implication, admitted, but it derives its force in part from the fact that the common term is a sensitivity to imaginative phenomena; also from the fact that this capacity, which itself is imaginative, calls for the ability to express a mastery of the iconography in some way that is appropriate both to the act of appreciation and to the social facts that are to be interpreted.

I can perhaps make this clearer by adverting to a more routine kind of work in anthropology. To make an effective analysis of a system of prescriptive alliance calls for specific knowledge about the history of ideas, conceptual criticism, known systems of the kind, hypothetical forms, probable correlations, structural principles of terminologies, and so on. This can be fairly demanding, and it calls for some intellectual finesse if it is to be done properly; but it can all be taught, step by step, and anyone who has gone about things in the right way can take on the analysis of a new prescriptive system. To a degree, in other words, this kind of work is methodical and even technical: it does not call for an "exceptional sensitivity and receptivity," but for much more workaday intellectual capacities.

Yet compare what is demanded in the interpretation of forms of the imagination. The repertory of factors is incomplete, there are no logical restrictions on the range of systems, there are no established principles of accretion, and in the nature of the material the precise combinations and their local meanings are unpredictable. A great deal depends therefore on an imaginative acuity such as is called for in the ultimate tests of translation. As if this were not enough, a matching ability is needed in rendering an ethnographical interpretation of what has been discerned, and this entails a literary artistry that cannot be had by academic training. At its highest, this enviable capacity is to be found, from my point of view, in George Eliot, Dostoevsky, and Gorky. In anthropology, a remarkable example is already famous under the title *The Teachings of Don Juan*, by Carlos Castañeda. Whatever professional misgivings may be entertained, on ethnographic grounds, this work in some regards exhibits the kind of gift that is peculiarly apt to an interpretation of the social forms assumed by characteristic themes and images. Those of us who cannot by their endowments attain such a pitch of sensibility combined with reportorial cogency — and that must mean most of us — have no realistic chance of elucidating alien forms of experience in the fashion that ideally is required by the imaginative demands of the task.

This is not a counsel of despair: it is a counsel of perfection. We have no right to think that an anthropologist should be capable of the supreme practice of a humane discipline, in the form of a radical and generalizable account of the psyche, any more than we could presume of a literate person that he should be capable of writing *Urne-Buriall* or *The Waste Land*. What I am urging rather is that we shall not do even our best until we rightly reassess our task and also the standards that will have to be kept in view if we are at all to succeed in it. We might for instance contemplate what social anthropology could become if ethnographic interpretations were ever written with the empathic penetration and the literary discipline of *Middlemarch* or *Things as They Are* or *Between the Acts*. This could not often be done, but never at all unless it were made an ambition. In that event we might at least have a chance to break free from an academic social anthropology that is increasingly bureaucratic and prudential; and then we might yet achieve something that would be found to possess the humane significance which at present is sought in the imaginative inventions of metaphysics and art.

Select Bibliography

Select Bibliography

Baal, J. van
    1977   Review of *Le Symbolisme en général*, by Dan Sperber. *Bijdragen tot de Taal-, Land- en Volkenkunde* 133:163–65.

Beidelman, T. O.
    1963   "Witchcraft in Ukaguru." In *Witchcraft and Sorcery in East Africa*, ed. John Middleton and E. H. Winter, pp. 57–98. London: Routledge and Kegan Paul.

Benveniste, Emile
    1966   *Problèmes de linguistique générale*. Paris: Presses Universitaires de France.

Clark, Kenneth
    1960   *The Nude: A Study of Ideal Art*. Harmondsworth, Middlesex: Penguin Books.

Durkheim, Emile
    1901   *Les Règles de la méthode sociologique*. 2d ed. Paris.

Durkheim, Emile, and Marcel Mauss
    1963   *Primitive Classification*. Translated from the French and edited with an introduction by Rodney Needham. Chicago: University of Chicago Press. (First published in French; Paris, 1903.)

Eliade, Mircea
    1964   *Shamanism: Archaic Techniques of Ecstasy*. Bollingen Series, 76. New York: Pantheon Books.

Freud, S.
    1973   *New Introductory Lectures on Psychoanalysis*. The Pelican

Freud Library, vol. 2. Harmondsworth, Middlesex:
Penguin Books.

Hampshire, Stuart
1959   *Thought and Action.* London: Chatto and Windus.

Hocart, A. M.
1970   *The Life-giving Myth.* Edited by Lord Raglan; second
impression, edited with a foreword by Rodney Needham. London: Methuen.

Jacobi, Jolande
1959   *Complex/Archetype/Symbol in the Psychology of C. G. Jung.*
Translated by Ralph Manheim. London: Routledge and
Kegan Paul.

Lafitau, Joseph François
1724   *Moeurs des sauvages amériquains comparées aux moeurs des pre-
miers temps.* 2 vols. Paris.

Lloyd, Geoffrey
1966   *Polarity and Analogy: Two Types of Argumentation in Early
Greek Thought.* Cambridge: At the University Press.

Mayer, Philip
1954   *Witches.* Inaugural Lecture, Rhodes University, Gra-
hamstown, South Africa. Reprinted in *Witchcraft and
Sorcery,* ed. Max Marwick, pp. 45–64. Harmondsworth,
Middlesex: Penguin Books, 1970.

Needham, Rodney
1972   *Belief, Language, and Experience.* Oxford: Basil Blackwell;
Chicago: University of Chicago Press.
1973   (ed.) *Right & Left: Essays on Dual Symbolic Classification.*
Chicago: University of Chicago Press.
1974   *Remarks and Inventions: Skeptical Essays about Kinship.* London: Tavistock; New York: Barnes & Noble.
1975   "Polythetic Classification." *Man,* n.s. 10:349–69.
1976   "Skulls and Causality." *Man,* n.s. 11:71–88.
1978   *Essential Perplexities.* Inaugural Lecture, University of
Oxford. Oxford: Clarendon Press.
1978   *Symbolic Classification.* Santa Monica, Calif.: Goodyear
Publishing Co.

Rycroft, Charles
    1975   "Freud and the Imagination." *New York Review*, 3 April, pp. 26–30.

Waismann, F.
    1968   *How I See Philosophy*. Edited by R. Harré. London: Macmillan.

Whitehead, Alfred North
    1927   *Symbolism: Its Meaning and Effect*. Cambridge: At the University Press.

Wittgenstein, Ludwig
    1967   *Zettel*. Oxford: Basil Blackwell.
    1969   *The Blue and Brown Books*. Oxford: Basil Blackwell.

Index

Index

Academics, 53, 69
Accretion, 44
Allendy, R., 10
Analysis, factorial, 19
Animal behavior, 4-5
Animal familiars, 38-39, 41
Animals, 53
Apollonius, 33, 63
Archetype, 45, 48
Art, 3, 60, 61, 62, 76
Aspect, change of, 33, 54
Attention, foci of, 18
Autonomy, 3, 68

Baal, Jan van, 59, 60
Bastian, Adolf, 19
Batak, 36
Beckett, Samuel, 70
Belief, 2, 8, 24
Benveniste, Emile, 20
Berkeley, William, 1
Black, 10, 37, 42
Blame, 32
Blessing, 27, 42, 62
Blood, 12
Blood offering, 19

Borneo, 19, 40, 70
Boundaries, 27, 35, 36
Brain, 47, 48, 49, 50, 66, 68, 73
Browne, Sir Thomas, 23, 76

Cannibalism, 33, 43
Cassirer, Ernst, 9
Castañeda, Carlos, 76
Categories, 20, 21, 52, 67
Cathexis, 72
Cause, 14, 43, 62
Cerebral functions, 48
Chekhov, Anton P., 70
Clark, Kenneth, 3
Classification, 15, 35, 38, 51,
    52; symbolic, 12, 13
Code, 13
Color, 9-10, 37, 38, 41, 46; see
    also Black; Red; White
Complementaries, 34
Complex, 18, 25, 60; as primary,
    42
Concern, social, 42, 43, 44
Condensation, 60
Consciousness, 2, 4, 13, 20, 48,

Consciousness (*cont.*)
67, 69, 73; disorderly
function of, 65
Constancy, 58
Constituents, elementary, 12, 21
Constraints, 3, 16, 17, 21, 50,
51, 68; abrogation of, 58,
59, 60; evasion of, 59, 61,
63, 64, 67, 71
Contradictions, 55, 56
Correlation, 15, 28
Crime, mystical, 50
Culture, 14, 64, 74
Cursing, 62

Darkness, 36, 41
de Vries, J., 10
Demetrius, 63
Descent: modes of, 17; systems,
16-17
Determinants, 15, 17, 21, 50,
67, 68
Disorder, 65, 67, 72
Domitian, 33
Dostoevsky, Fëdor M., 75
Dreams, 45, 64, 71, 72, 73, 74
Drugs, 43
Dürer, Albrecht, 40
Durkheim, Emile, 3, 47, 58, 66,
68

Ego, 71
Egypt, 39
Elementargedanken, 19
Eliade, Mircea, 19
Eliot, George, 75
Emotions, 68, 74

Energy, psychical, 72
Enlightenment, the, 5
Epistemology, 21
Experience, human, 7, 14, 20,
28, 44, 45, 46, 51, 65, 66,
68, 76

Fantasy, 45, 60, 70, 72
Fear, 43, 44, 62
Features, characteristic, 14;
of myth, 57, 60, 65, 67, 69,
71; of totemism, 51, 52; of
the witch, 44
Fence, 27
Fiction, 60
Flight, 39-40, 41, 43, 64
Freedom, 4, 20, 21, 67, 68
Freud, Sigmund, 65, 70, 72-73

Genetics, 49
Gorky, Maxim, 76
Granary, 30
Gurung, 37

Half man, 19
Hallucinations, 43
Head, detached, 40
Hemispheres, cerebral, 48, 69
Heraldry, 38
Heroes, 43, 58
Hertz, R., 34
Hindu, 39
Hocart, A. M., 40
Homology, 55

Iconography, 74, 75
Id, 70, 71, 72, 73

Imagination, 33, 36, 40, 44, 47, 51, 59, 68, 75; collective modes of, 71, 72; limits to, 50, 65, 67; neglect of, 65; predispositions of, 60, 67; and social facts, 66; vagrancy of, 64, 69, 70; vectors of, 2
Immediacy, 11, 12, 21, 64
Impossibility, 59, 61
Inattention, 73
Incest, 33, 42
Inconstancy, 58, 59, 60, 64, 71
Individualism, 20, 50, 67
Innate ideas, 18
Inner state, 24, 25
Intellectualism, 51, 53, 65, 66, 70
Intention, 60
Inversion, 35, 36, 41

Jefferson, Thomas, 1
Jung, C. G., 45, 66

Kafka, Franz, 58
Kaguru, 35, 37
Kalapalo, 39
Kings, 40

Lafitau, Joseph François, 16
Lang, Andrew, 55
Language, ideal, 18
Leader, religious, 63
Lévy-Bruhl, Lucien, 61
Light, 36
Lloyd, Geoffrey, E. R., 9

Logic, 15, 16, 17, 18, 21, 50, 52, 55, 59, 61, 64, 70, 75
Lowie, R. H., 16
Luck, 31
Lugbara, 35

Mauss, Marcel, 58
Mayer, Philip, 28
Meaning, 6, 11, 12, 18, 46, 62-63, 73, 75; see also Semantic units
Metamorphosis, 58, 59, 64, 71
Metaphor, 9, 23, 35, 36, 41, 44, 48
Metaphysics, 4, 6, 9, 76
Mind, human, 55, 56
Miracles, 63
Misfortune, theory of, 30-32
Mugwe, 37
Myth, theories of, 55, 56, 57; see also Features, characteristic

"Natural kinds," 18
Nature, human, 7, 8, 47, 65, 66, 67
Negative capability, 74
Night, 36, 37
Nocturnal lights, 41, 43
Numbers, 10
Nyoro, 10

Occam, William of, 72
Oedipus, 58
Opposite, 34, 36
Opposition, 15, 34, 35, 41, 48, 55
Ovid, 58

Percussion, 10-11, 48
Petrouchka, 62
Philosophy, empirical, 7
Physics, 40
Pinter, Harold, 70
Polarities, 34
Polythetic combination, 33, 41, 43, 67
Power, malign, 28, 40
Prayer, 42
Predicates, ultimate, 20
Predictions, 58
Prejudice, 27, 28
Prescriptive (alliance) systems, 2, 15, 65, 75
Principles, 17
Processes, primary/secondary, 70, 72
Proclivities, 17, 21, 36, 44, 51, 54, 67, 72
Properties, 57, 60, 63
Psyche, 65, 66, 72, 76
Psychoanalysis, 70
Psychology: depth, 46; formal, 47
Purum, 15

Rationality, 62, 66, 69
"Real character," 18, 20
Reality, 13, 28, 44, 61, 62, 68
Reason, 50, 61, 69
Red, 10, 12, 48
Relations, 14, 15, 48
Repertory, 42, 46
Repression, 71
Resemblances: family, 57; natural, 13, 18; sporadic, 33, 41

Resistance, 72, 73
Right/left, 12, 14-15, 34, 35, 46
Ritual, 62, 65
Rycroft, Charles, 74

Sacrifice, 19
Saints, 34, 40, 42, 63
Science, 4, 6, 7, 11, 25
Semantic units, 12-13, 14, 15, 46, 73
Sex, 72
Shamanism, 19, 37, 40, 42, 43, 62, 63
Sin, 31
Sorcerer, 25-26
Sound, 10, 46
Space, 59, 72
Stone, 19
Strains, 28
Stress, 32
Structural analysis, 15, 55, 56
Structuralism, 6
Sublimation, 29
Symmetry, 15
Synthesis, 42, 43, 45, 46, 48, 49
Syzygies, 34

Theory, 6, 12, 14, 32, 55, 56, 57
Thought, 15, 51, 70; Greek, 9
Time, 59, 62, 72
Totemism, 12, 38, 51, 52, 53
Transformation, 55
Transition, 11, 60
Transitivity, 15
Translation, 75
Transposition, 55, 64, 71

Trevor-Roper, Hugh R., 30
Trobrianders, 41
Tropism, 48
Turnpikes, 25
Typology, 16, 26, 57, 66

Unconscious, the, 45, 65, 72

Vectors, 2, 48
Virginia, Commonwealth of, 1, 2, 68
Vocabularies, 8, 10

Waismann, F., 66
White, 10, 37, 42

Whitehead, Alfred North, 1
Wićća, 27; *see also* Witch
Will, 4, 17, 20, 21, 41, 65, 67
Wishes, 71, 73
Witch, 23-50, 60, 62, 63
Witchcraft, accusations of, 28-29, 30
Wittgenstein, Ludwig, 49, 56, 70
Wizard, 26, 27

Yogis, 40

Zeus, 58

The University of Virginia Lectures on Individual and Society

The Committee on Comparative Study of Individual and Society and the Center for Advanced Studies, University of Virginia, together sponsor occasional lectures intended to deepen understanding of the complex and vital issues embedded in the interrelationships between the individual and society.